The Complete
Do-It-Yourself Guide
to Business Plans

2020 Edition

Your Uncle Ralph

Delvin R. Chatterson

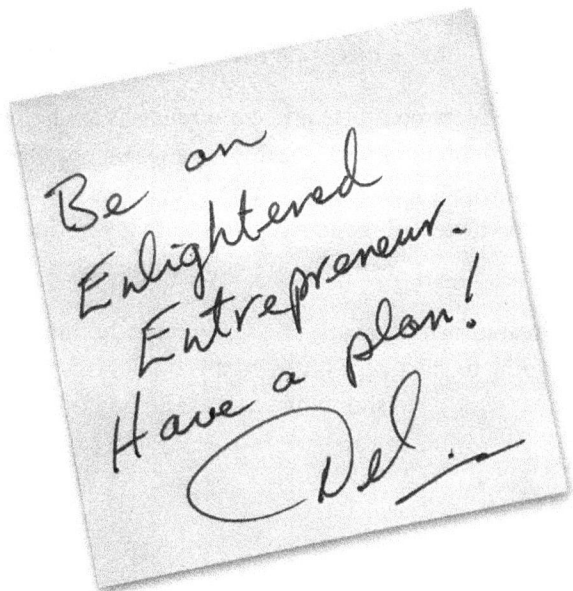

*Be an
Enlightered
Entrepreneur.
Have a plan!
Del*

For entrepreneurs from *your Uncle Ralph*, Delvin R. Chatterson:

Don't Do It the Hard Way

"A wise man learns from the mistakes of others. Only a fool insists on making his own."

Sharing stories of experienced entrepreneurs to learn how to avoid the mistakes and grow a successful business.

For more from Del Chatterson and your Uncle Ralph visit the websites or join the mailing lists at:

LearningEntrepreneurship.com

DelvinChatterson.com

Or follow him on social media:

- Facebook: Author – Delvin Chatterson
- Instagram: Delvin R. Chatterson, Author
- LinkedIn: Del Chatterson
- Twitter: @ Del_UncleRalph

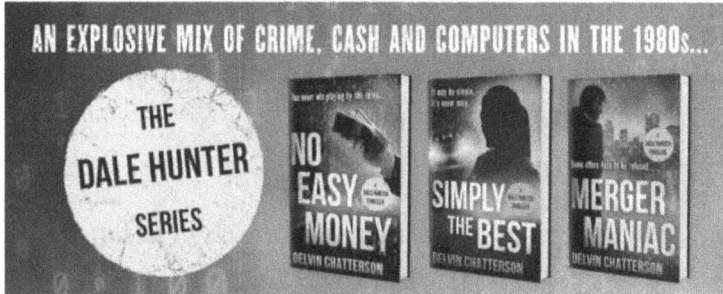

AN EXPLOSIVE MIX OF CRIME, CASH AND COMPUTERS IN THE 1980s...

THE DALE HUNTER SERIES

No Easy Money

You never win playing by the rules...

First in the series of Dale Hunter crime novels, No Easy Money is an explosive mix of crime, cash and computers in the 1980s. Dale Hunter is a young entrepreneur in the computer business under threats of violence from the Montreal Mafia. He wants to survive and not play by gangster rules, but it will require courage and creativity and the support of some new friends. Somebody is going to get killed.

Simply the Best

It may be simple, it's never easy

Dale Hunter is back in business, but so is Gino Boncanno. Hunter has already had to save himself from a murder attempt by the gangster, Boncanno. Now his new partner in Taiwan introduces him to the Triads and their smuggling schemes into the U.S. The danger escalates and Hunter still has to save himself and his family from the murderous plans of Boncanno. It may be simple, but it's never easy.

Merger Maniac

Some offers have to be refused

Third in the series, Merger Maniac is the story of how Dale Hunter is trying to thrive in the rapidly evolving computer business of the 1980s. He's looking for merger partners, but has to escape the aggressive and violent Montreal Mafia, who want him to join their money laundering schemes and are making very persuasive offers. Hunter has to walk a dangerous tightrope to avoid using their dirty money and getting dragged into more crime and corruption.

High Praise For
The Dale Hunter Series

"Chatterson's language conveys mayhem with a brevity that practically demands attention. Action sequences are rapid fire and corrosive … offset by threatening undertones. Chatterson pens crime drama that is fast-paced and involved."

INDIE READER REVIEW

"Great read! … I had to get up in the middle of the night to finish it!"

KEN COLLINS (CANADA)

"I read this book in one day … How do I get my hands on his next book?"

MARGARET HEATON (USA)

Amazing! An absolutely outstanding writer! Hooked and thoroughly entertained. …. a captivating author."

PETER J. MALOUF (CANADA)

"I liked it a lot! And I was there, in the computer business of the 1980s. I'm telling all my friends, very impressive!"

GILLES GAUDET (CANADA)

"Welcome to the '80s Business World. I love how the story flowed and the intensity continued to increase, keeping you reading to the very end. Keeps you on the edge of your seat for an intense and exciting read. Enjoy the ride! It's a fast one!"

AMANDA LEEBER (USA), AMAZON.COM REVIEW

"Loved it right from the beginning! The passion felt between the characters had me not wanting to put it down. A definite must read! Looking forward to reading book two."

JASMIN MOORE, GOODREADS REVIEWER

The Complete Do-It-Yourself Guide to Business Plans

Get the results you want

2020 EDITION

Your Uncle Ralph

Delvin R. Chatterson

The Complete Do-It-Yourself Guide to Business Plans
2020 Edition

ISBN softcover: 978-0-9879569-1-0
ISBN EPUB: 978-0-9879569-2-7
ISBN MOBI: 978-0-9879569-3-4

Advance release – March 2020
Final release – June 2020

Disclaimer: Throughout this Guide and in the Real life Stories, the actual individual names and business details have been changed to protect the identity of the subjects of each story. Any apparent use of real names is purely coincidental.

For volume purchases or quantity discounts please contact the Author or Publisher directly.

Published by:
Uncle Ralph's Publishing Empire
(A division of 146152 Canada Inc.)
LearningEntrepreneurship.com
&
Canam Books/Rapido Press

Dedicated to the principle that enlightened entrepreneurs
do better for themselves and their businesses
by also doing better for their families and employees,
their customers, suppliers and business partners,
their communities and the planet.

Be better. Do better.

Can *Uncle Ralph* help you?

As a cautious and skeptical entrepreneur, and before you spend your valuable time and money on this 2020 edition of **The Complete Do-It-Yourself Guide to Business Plans**, you should be asking whether it is going to give you the results you want.

How can Del Chatterson, *your Uncle Ralph,* help with your Business Plan? What does he know? Who has he helped and how? You have a right to know.

To answer those questions, here's what bankers and clients have said about working with me, and the Business Plans we've done together:

- *"Very well done! This answers all our questions and I can get approval quickly for you."* Lending officer, CIBC Bank.

- *"This is exactly what we like to see in a Business Plan."* Account Manager, Business Development Bank of Canada.

- *"Now we have a documented strategy and financial projections that help us understand the business potential and take it to the next level."* Partners in a marketing services business.

- *"Finally we have a plan we can work with. Thanks, Del, we never would have made it without you."* Two experienced executives launching a freight brokerage business.

- *"I would not hesitate to recommend Del to anyone seeking professional guidance in making their business grow."* Owner, Retail Business.

- *"Del respects and understands the entrepreneur. He led us to focus on the most important issues."* Entrepreneur, Office Furniture.

- *"His experience and expertise were utilized to develop a bullet-proof business plan. The plan will certainly attract new investors."* President, Procurement Services Business.

- *"Hey Del, they liked the Plan and we're getting the loans!"* Entrepreneurs purchasing a garage and car wash business.

I expect to hear the same happy feedback from you after you read the Complete Do-It-Yourself Guide and apply it to your own Business Plans.

It will make a difference for you and your business.
The process will be easier and you'll get the results you want.

GUIDE TO THE CONTENTS

APPENDICES

Introduction to your *Uncle Ralph*

You may still be wondering, "Who is Uncle Ralph and how can he help me prepare a business plan that gets the results I want?"

So here is my story. I am your Uncle Ralph. You can call me Del.

I'm an experienced business advisor, writer and cheerleader for entrepreneurs. A consultant, executive, entrepreneur, writer, golfer and photographer. I also play hockey and guitar. I am recently re-married and have an extended family, including two adult kids and two grandsons. I am originally a small town boy from the Rocky Mountains of British Columbia in western Canada; now living in the fascinating, multicultural, bilingual, French-Canadian city of Montreal.

My background is Engineer from UBC in Vancouver with an MBA from McGill in Montreal with extensive experience as a corporate executive, management consultant, entrepreneur and business owner. My corporate experience included financial analysis and systems integration projects, purchasing and materials management. In management consulting, I was six years with Coopers and Lybrand working with businesses across Canada and in Europe and Central America.

With my own consulting business, DirectTech Solutions, I have worked as a business consultant with many entrepreneurs, including clients of the Business Development Bank of Canada (BDC), in a wide variety of industries. Clients were at different stages of their business life cycle from start-up to exit and facing challenges that ranged from strategic leadership and management direction on cash flow issues to performance improvement in operations, sales and marketing.

As an entrepreneur, I was eight years growing a distribution business, TTX Computer Products, from zero to $20 million per year. I then spent three years taking it into and then out of a merger with another Canadian computer products distributor.

Your Uncle Ralph has learned from my own experience and from observations of all the good and bad managers that I have worked with over the years. Coincidentally, Ralph is my secret middle name and was my father's first name. Uncle Ralph is definitely much wiser than I am and has experienced more than I could possibly have lived through myself.

Uncle Ralph is dedicated to sharing his ideas, experience and advice with other executives, entrepreneurs and managers to help improve their businesses and the lives of everyone around them. Of course, I will also learn something in the process and look forward to sharing that with you, too.

MY BUSINESS PLANNING STORY

It started with a few ideas scratched out on paper with a rough budget that showed how we might actually be able to make money in a regional distribution business for computer hardware. The company was called TTX Computer Products. Nobody cared about it at that stage, except me and my partner. *That's usually the first and best reason to prepare a Business Plan – to help the owners direct their decision making and action plans.*

We each put in a few thousand dollars and launched the business in April of 1986 with two employees. The first month we did $10,000 in sales. Not a bad start. (Even if I did keep the books open for an extra few days just to meet our objective.) We were profitable from the third month. And we kept profitable and growing over the next eight years until the business exceeded $20 million in annual sales.

With each stage of growth we needed additional financing. To get started, the bank said, "It sounds OK, but we need two things – your personal guarantees and a business plan."

So we signed the personal guarantees and I updated and expanded our initial Business Plan – added a few more pages and some financial projections. It was good enough to get us the first $50,000. The loans grew with the business until, with the merger in 1994, we were up to $4.8 million in bank lines of credit *with no personal guarantees.*

That's what a well-documented Business Plan can do for you. (Of course, a good track record of profitable growth also helps.)

My next start-up venture was an e-commerce business with a technology partner. This time we prepared more elaborate Business Plans to support the "dot-com" business model with high development costs, rapid customer acquisition and low revenues for the first few years and millions required in venture capital funding to get us to global domination. (We were both ambitious and optimistic at the start.)

We received great response to our Business Plan, negotiated deals with important strategic partners (another key use for your Business Plan), finished the development work, launched and started growing the business. When the dot-com bubble burst, however, we learned a lot more about business planning and managing financing on the downside. We also learned when it was time to give up and move on with a new plan.

Over more than two decades in my consulting business, I have worked with many different entrepreneurs and their investors to develop, evaluate, prepare and present Business Plans that delivered results. I have also given courses in Business Planning at Concordia University in Montreal to help new entrepreneurs get their businesses started.

In recent years, I have gained more international business exposure working as a Volunteer Advisor with Canadian Executive Services

Overseas (CESO), an agency providing aid to countries in developing economies around the world and to aboriginal communities in Canada. It has been an enlightening experience to share my ideas and solutions with entrepreneurs who are facing the additional obstacles of high rates of poverty, mostly untrained workers and limited or ineffective supporting infrastructure.

All this history and experience has been incorporated into writing this comprehensive reference for entrepreneurs, **The Complete Do-It-Yourself Guide to Business Plans**.

Please make good use of it for your own plans. I look forward to hearing of your success in achieving the results you want.

Good luck and happy planning!

Your Uncle Ralph
Del Chatterson

Introduction to the Complete Do-It-Yourself Guide to Business Plans

2020 EDITION

Get the results you want

Preparing a Business Plan remains an important and necessary requirement for every business. For most business owners it is not an easy task.

Even with this Do-It-Yourself Guide you will find that you need the assistance of others – your banker or accountant, a consultant or your business associates. And certainly your partners and senior management team, once you have them.

But this Guide will help you to get the most out of the process and prepare a Business Plan that gets the results that you want – for a business start-up, new financing, growth and profitability, even sale and exit from the business, when you are at that stage.

Every entrepreneur needs to prepare and regularly refer to a current and relevant documented business plan to provide direction to the management team and help them deliver the desired performance and results.

But most importantly, I want to emphasize throughout:

The primary value in preparing a solid business plan comes from the process, not the product.

More than a document, your business plan is an important management tool to build and grow a successful business.

The product is a valuable and necessary document, but the real value to the entrepreneur will be in the process of assessing the marketing opportunities, developing business strategies, testing marketing and operating plans, and evaluating the expected financial results under alternative scenarios.

This process (if well done, according to the methods that I will describe in this Guide) will lead you to prepare a plan for the business that is realistic, achievable, well understood and supported by all of the stakeholders involved – owners, managers, staff, lenders and investors.

My intent is to provide everything you need to "do-it-yourself" and prepare your own Business Plan, but you will also learn how to direct other participants in the process – your staff and your consultants or advisors. This comprehensive Guide will cover all the aspects of completing a successful business plan.

You will know that your plan is successful when it meets two key criteria:

1. **It helps you get the financing you need, and**

2. **It leads you to building and growing a profitable business.**

We will discuss the purpose of doing a business plan; choices of different business concepts, financial structures and strategies; business plan content, style and layout; and how to prepare a complete set of financial projections.

The Complete Do-It-Yourself Guide to Business Plans is a consolidation of everything that I have learned from the preparation and analysis of dozens of business plans as an entrepreneur, executive, and consultant. It incorporates the best practices that I have found over the past thirty years to achieve the desired results for business owners.

My objective with this 2020 edition is to provide an expanded and enhanced version of the Guide based on readers' feedback from the First Edition of 2010 and the Second Edition published in 2014. This edition includes new material, more real-life stories, expanded sample Business Plans with corresponding financial projections and additional examples for The Pitch and The Exit, plus valuable ideas, tools, tactics and techniques to help you prepare a better Business Plan.

In addition to this guide you should take advantage of the advice from Uncle Ralph at LearningEntrepreneurship.com and sign-up for the Ideas for Entrepreneurs newsletter for occasional updates and new ideas, information and inspiration.

If you apply all that you learn, I am confident that you will get great value out of the process; as well as prepare a dynamite business plan that gets you the results you want.

Learn by doing it!

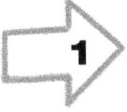

What is a Business Plan?

What are the results you want?

A business plan is a document that describes your idea for realizing a business opportunity. It describes the market need that you have identified and the proposed strategies and plans to turn your idea into a profitable business.

The business plan is a communications tool to be used with all the prospective participants in your project. It will identify and confirm the business opportunity, define your proposed business model for responding to that opportunity and describe the strategies, operating plans and financial results that you expect.

It is not exactly a sales document, but it will be used to sell your concept and approach to convince sources of financing and strategic business partners to participate in your plan.

An acceptable Business Plan will include a detailed and comprehensive description of the planned project or new venture with extensive financial analysis and projections, plus supporting material that might include executive profiles, product brochures, facilities plans and market research studies.

The three key components in a Business Plan therefore, are:

1. A clear, persuasive description of the business opportunity and your strategies and action plans to respond to it.

2. A complete detailed set of financial projections confirming the investment required and the expected future profitability.

3. Supporting documentation that confirms the objective research and analysis for the conclusions, proposals and projections shown in the plan.

The Complete Do-It-Yourself Guide to Business Plans will explain:

- How to prepare all the elements required for a complete business plan package

- How to get the most out of the process

- How to get the results you want.

Why Do You Need a Business Plan?

It has a purpose.

The most common reason for preparing a business plan is, "because the bank asked for one." That is probably why most readers of this Guide are here. And that is obviously a legitimate reason for doing one.

But why is the bank asking for one? And do you need one for the same reasons?

The answer is as simple as the familiar cliché: If you fail to plan; you plan to fail.

It's hard to know where you're going and how you're getting there without a plan. It's even harder to manage your progress if you haven't defined your destination and set the milestones to monitor along the way. What route are you taking? What type of vehicle are you using? Who's driving and who are the passengers? Why?

The bank, and any other investor or business partner, wants the answers to those questions to assess whether or not you are likely to succeed and whether or not they want to support you.

You need a business plan for all the same reasons.

Every business needs one, from the start-up to the exit.

Documenting a Business Plan is an extremely useful process to focus the owners and the management team on their business model, strategies, and operating plans. The process will force consensus and decision making that might otherwise be neglected. It requires issues to be resolved and the conclusions to be documented after testing alternative solutions and their financial consequences.

A well-documented business plan will help you communicate the most important elements of your strategy and plans to the people who need to know them the most. Including you.

Maybe you've been successful in business for many years and never had a business plan. It's still a good idea for all the same reasons. And now is a good time.

Maybe you're ready to exit your business. Even better. A solid business plan will be the most important document you have to support the value of your business for sale or transfer to a new owner.

The greatest value of a business plan, however, is always in the process — involving your management team in a thorough examination of your business; its purpose, its strategies and its plans to ensure success. When it's completed, all the key players will be more knowledgeable of the issues, the opportunities, the risks and the alternative paths considered and the reasons for the choices that were made; before committing to the final plan.

For a small business start-up, that management team may only be you. Maybe you'd rather keep your plans to yourself. But the business plan is still a valuable exercise. It forces you to answer all the questions that you should ask yourself and that will certainly be asked by the next people to get involved.

With a well-documented business plan you will be better prepared to meet all the challenges and more likely to succeed.

Real Life Story: "Don't take that to the bank"

It started with, "Hi Del, we found you on the Internet."

A week later, I was sitting down with Peter, Paul and Mary to work with them on their start-up business plan.

Peter and Paul were two experienced executives in the computer service business and Mary was Paul's wife. They wanted to quit their current jobs and start their own business that would succeed where their current employers were failing. They had the necessary knowledge, experience and contacts to quickly get up to speed and immediately win business from their competitors.

But there were two major flaws in their initial plan. First, they had an unnamed additional partner who was currently the Purchasing Agent with a customer of their current employer. He was promising to switch a large contract from that company to the new business. Oops! Probably a firing offense as a conflict of interest for the silent partner and a breach of the employment or non-competition agreements signed by Peter and Paul with their current employer. We agreed to leave the silent partner out of the deal, at least while he remained in his current job. The new business owners would also have to be careful how they approached past customers of their current employer to avoid provoking any legal challenges.

The second major flaw in their plan was their intention to attract both suppliers and customers with very generous terms of payment. The exact opposite of the recommended cash management policy to "collect fast and pay slow," they intended to let their customers pay slow and to pay their suppliers fast. Certainly attractive for both their customers and their suppliers, but a disaster for their own financing and profitability.

Not something to take to the bank to demonstrate good management and a plan for success.

So we reverted to normal industry payment terms in the plan and focused on their strengths of industry knowledge and technical expertise to attract customers and suppliers instead of the potentially risky strategy of overly generous payment terms. That not only made the plan more presentable, but it also reduced the start-up financing requirement from over $100,000 to less than $40,000.

These were valuable changes to their business plan resulting from the process of testing strategies and plans to see the real impact on operations and financial results. They then succeeded in financing the business with a supportive and confident bank. Two years later they were growing fast.

(Note: In all these Real life Stories, the actual names and business details have been changed to protect the confidentiality of the businesses and their owners. Their stories are shared here for the express purpose of helping other entrepreneurs get better results from their Business Plans.)

What is the Process?

Recycle: Rethink, Review and Rewrite.

A few years ago, while revising my lecture material for a course on business planning at Concordia University in Montreal, I spent some time reviewing other resources available from a wide variety of sources. It was all very *uninspiring*.

Unconvincing in the reasons for doing a good business plan and entirely discouraging in describing the elaborate process for preparing one. Not likely to persuade busy, results-oriented, document-challenged entrepreneurs that they really needed a business plan and that they could do it for themselves.

My mission became clearer. I started to describe my own approach as: **Recycling your Business Plan**.

That is the process I recommend. Start with a very simple document, a one-page summary, then continuously review, revise and expand your plan to deal with more issues and answer more questions.

I'm reminded of the "million dollar napkin" that one entrepreneur boasts he used to start his business; simply responding to the challenge to write his plan on a restaurant napkin. And there are the thousands of successful businesses that were launched on the back of an envelope or on a notepad.

It's a good way to start your business plan.

Describe it in a few words on one page.

Can you answer these questions clearly and concisely?

- What is the purpose of your business?
- Who are the target customers?
- What is the investment required to get started?
- What is the revenue required to be profitable?
- How soon will you get there?

Simple questions that you need to be prepared to answer in every conversation about your business plan. Don't start until you have them sorted out in your head and the answers are scratched out on one page.

Remember the objective is to develop a strategic planning document to serve as a resource for communicating your plans for the business and as a guide for management to build and grow a profitable and successful business.

RECYCLING YOUR BUSINESS PLAN

When you are ready to start, here are the steps that I recommend to recycle your business plan. Each step leads to a revised version of your Business Plan that becomes more solid and convincing with each recycling:

1. **The Pitch:** On one page, or napkin, or envelope. (See the Appendix for examples.) Describe the market opportunity, your concept and business strategy to attract target customers, and the reasons you will succeed. Make it memorable with a company name and a marketing slogan.

2. **Confirm** that your **personal objectives** are consistent with your business objectives and that you have the **personality, skills, knowledge, experience and contacts** required to succeed. (Or explain how you will acquire them.)

3. **Collect and analyse data** on your market, target customers and primary competitors. Confirm the market opportunity and that your strategy will meet customer needs better than competitive alternatives and other solutions.

4. Do a **feasibility test** at your estimated sales volumes, pricing and operating costs to determine profitability. Calculate the break-even sales level and compare it to your forecasts. Revise and re-calculate until you can confirm sales forecasts that will exceed the break-even and deliver sustainable profitability.

5. **Document in more detail** your business concept and the plans for facilities, organisation, operations, marketing and sales. Add a section on the risks considered and your planned response to anything that may not go according to plan.

6. **Expand the financial analysis** to include start-up investment costs, including working capital, and the cash flow forecasts to determine the financing required. How much is required and when? How and when will it be repaid? Test alternative scenarios to ensure that potential variations in sales forecasts and cost estimates still lead to profitability and that the financing secured will be adequate until you get there.

7. **Complete the business plan and a full set of financial projections:** Use the outline and checklist of requirements for your intended audience — senior management, lenders, investors, or strategic partners — and add relevant supporting documentation.

8. **Recycle** the essential elements to capture your Business Plan in a two-to-three page Executive Summary, in a 1-minute elevator pitch, and in a 10-20 slide PowerPoint presentation for alternate forms of introduction to your plan.

9. The final recycling step for your Business Plan is to continuously **re-use it** to monitor, manage and improve your future operating results. Check whether the plan and the objectives are still valid and then revise your plans or improve your performance to achieve the updated objectives.

That's it.
Recycling is good.

Those few simple steps will take you from a good idea to a well-developed and fully documented Business Plan that will persuade others to invest in your plan and will serve as your guide for managing performance to achieve the results you intended.

Real Life Story: "Do-It-Yourself is the way to go."

My partner and I had decided that we had a world class business idea that could be a huge success story for us and any investors we could persuade to join us.

Our pitch was to build an online computer products distribution business that would serve the rapidly growing business and consumer market and apply web-based technologies that were becoming more efficient and affordable. (This was early 2000s before Google and Amazon conquered the world of search engines and e-commerce.)

Our business model would require significant development costs and might take years of investment before becoming profitable and self-sustaining. So we thought we needed an exceptionally good business plan prepared by professionals.

I said to my partner, "OK, I'll talk to my old friends at Coopers & Lybrand Management Consultants." I went to their expensively furnished offices in a large downtown office tower and met with a strategic planning consultant. He was quick to conclude, "You're better off to do it yourself."

I sat back and listened, as he explained. "First, our strategic planning mandates have a minimum fee of $50,000. Second, the more you pay for consultants the less believable the business plan is to outsiders. They're convinced that if you need expensive consultants to prepare and defend your plan, you probably cannot deliver on it yourself either."

That was pretty clear and entirely appropriate for us. We didn't want to invest as much as $50,000 in the business plan and we needed to work on it ourselves. We learned a lot in the process that we might have missed if we had delegated it all to the high-powered management consultants.

I became a strong believer in the value of the do-it-yourself business plan. I recommended that approach to other entrepreneurs and it led me to the first edition of the Do-It-Yourself Guide to share what I had learned.

Even if you use the 2020 Edition, you may still decide to use outside professionals and consultants in the process. You may even be willing to pay their exorbitant fees, but you will be a more knowledgeable client and better able to guide them to deliver a business plan that gets the results you want.

4 ▷ Check Your Personal Objectives First

Do you really want to be your own boss? Do you have what it takes?

Before you make the leap into starting your own business, ask yourself these four questions:

- Is it a good personal career choice?
- What do I need to know to decide?
- How can I prepare myself?
- How do I get started?

In this section, I will help you find the answers to those key questions and understand the factors that determine who will succeed and who will not? Why and why not? What can you do to improve your prospects for success?

I often make the analogy that starting your own business is a lot like sky-diving — it seems like an exciting idea, but you're not likely to actually try it unless you're pushed out the door.

So what's pushing you?

In my case, I had literally been pushed out the door of a company that was winding down and my number finally came up. Not a surprise, since I had spent the previous nine months closing facilities and letting people go; but a painful experience, nevertheless. Two other corporate job offers were soon presented to me, but I decided that it was time to take care of my own career plan and not let someone else decide what I was doing next. Sound familiar to you?

Besides, with an MBA and lots of experience, I was ready to prove that I was at least as good a manager and businessman as the "idiots" I had been working for. That might sound a little arrogant or angry, but it did keep me motivated through the early setbacks.

How about you? Do you really want to own a business? Be your own boss?

The advantages are attractive, but don't forget the disadvantages that are an inevitable part of the choice. Consider both and check off those that are most appealing to you and those that are most discouraging. Compare and decide if you are still in favour of starting your own business. Is it a go or no-go?

The checklists for you to evaluate:

ADVANTAGES
- ❑ Unlimited opportunity to grow
- ❑ Personal freedom, independence
- ❑ Continuous challenge and variety
- ❑ Your choice of management style
- ❑ Responsibility for and involved in the whole business
- ❑ If the business does well, you do well

DISADVANTAGES
- ❑ There are still limits to what you can do or control
- ❑ New pressures from more people, who are now dependent on you
- ❑ Requirements for skills and knowledge you do not have
- ❑ You cannot leave it at the office
- ❑ Higher risks and a less secure financial future
- ❑ If the business fails, it will be tougher to find a "real" job

To keep it all in perspective, here are some comments by entrepreneurs to remind you what it means to be your own boss:

"I used to work for someone that I called boss. Now I work for thirty people who call me boss."

"I wanted to be my own boss. But now I have many bosses — my customers, my employees, my suppliers, the bank, the landlord, the government and the city! It's hard to satisfy them all."

"It's still better than working for somebody else."

"I'm the best boss I ever had!"

Which of those comments will apply to you and your business? Is it what you want?

And the most important question to ask yourself:

Am I likely to succeed?

So the next steps require some self-analysis and assessing whether you are the entrepreneurial type. First, let's agree that there is no easily identifiable entrepreneurial type. While it may be true that anyone can be an entrepreneur, there are certain personal characteristics, preferences, attitudes and abilities that are essential to success.

You need to honestly assess each of these key factors if you want to improve your chances to succeed as an entrepreneur. Complete this checklist before you go any further with your business plans.

- ❏ Are you more comfortable in the corporate or the entrepreneurial world?
- ❏ Do you seek and prefer a variety of challenges in your work and broader responsibilities beyond your area of expertise.
- ❏ How important are your needs for recognition and compensation.
- ❏ Do have particular personal strengths and weaknesses. Will they help or hurt the business?

❏ Are your education, training, available resources and contact network directly relevant to your planned business venture?

❏ Do you have these typical characteristics of successful entrepreneurs:
  • Independent, confident, self-reliant
  • Passionate, persistent, patient, determined
  • Action-oriented, risk taker
  • Effective communicator
  • Leader, achiever and team player.

❏ Is your supporting foundation solid – family, physical, and financial? Are they a distraction?

❏ Are important strategic relationships already in place – business partners, investors, suppliers, key customers and initial employees?

❏ Is the timing right? Now or never? Too soon or too late?

Does an honest evaluation of all these factors confirm that entrepreneurship is the right career choice for you? These questions and your answers will help you decide if you are ready to develop a plan to succeed in your chosen business venture.

Choosing the right opportunity that is a good fit for you and your personal objectives is the next step.

Real Life Story: "Don't quit your day job, yet."

Many young daydreamers and older ones that should know better, see entre-preneurship as their escape from a day job that is not meeting their needs.

"Surely, running my own business would be better than this!"

Well, maybe not. The same reasons that you are not succeeding on the job may also be big obstacles to your success in business. And entrepreneurship will test skills and capabilities that you have not tested before.

Consider the senior IBM sales executive who retired early and bought a hot dog franchise. He probably used none of his skills and experience from IBM and then also discovered he did not have the patience or aptitude to manage low-skill employees serving low-budget customers. It was neither a good investment nor a good decision for his next career.

Or consider the frustrated young computer technician, who wanted to start a business selling to all those home office users that needed his expertise instead of working for a demanding network services company with big corporate clients who never appreciated him enough. We chatted about his plans to quit and start his own business. He wanted to pay me to help him write a business plan that would get him started with a bank loan so he could pay himself until he found some customers and signed some contracts.

Sounds simple, right? But no bank would ever finance that plan. I had to persuade him to stop daydreaming; keep his money and keep his day job.

A better plan was to upgrade his technical skills and get some experience in management and sales with his current employer, so that he could then launch his own business in the same attractive corporate services environment. Too many unhappy computer technicians have already been under-employed and under-paid trying to service the difficult home office and consumer market. It's better to upgrade your expertise and qualifications and offer your services to higher paying corporate and institutional clients who will appreciate the higher value services that you can provide.

Look before you leap.

5 Find the Right Business Opportunity

Make it personal, do it differently.

If you have now satisfactorily confirmed that you have what it takes to succeed as an entrepreneur and you are determined to proceed, then you need to identify and qualify the business opportunity which best meets your entrepreneurial ambitions. It is essential that your choice leverages your personal knowledge, skills, experience and contacts into a successful and sustainable business.

Those are the appropriately defined criteria to select the right business opportunity for you. The selection process will require focus and hard work. No more daydreaming about how you would like to be rich and famous.

Be realistic about your skills, talents, education and experience for the business venture that you choose. You would not be the first high-powered corporate executive that failed at running a restaurant franchise. Is your past success transferrable?

Build on what you already know you can do and add what's missing with good strategic partnerships, management, employees, professional advisors and suppliers.

Your search and selection of a suitable potential business opportunity starts with your **personal knowledge, experience and contacts**. The choice will then be defined and refined by doing your homework.

Yes, your "gut feel" and intuition are important, but let's balance the feelings with the facts.

These the important initial questions that need to be answered:

- ❏ Which opportunities match my capabilities?
- ❏ What is the specific market need, deficiency or problem that I can solve?
- ❏ What current solutions are available?
- ❏ What other options does the customer have?
- ❏ What is my proposed solution?
- ❏ Has the appeal of my solution been confirmed by market testing and customer feedback?
- ❏ Can I deliver the solution and make it profitable?

MARKET RESEARCH

A very important start is to do basic market research into the target markets, current competitors and potential customers. Market research will give you important quantitative and qualitative data on each of the following:

- ❏ The most attractive segments, customers and opportunities.
- ❏ Growth potential – a growing market offers more opportunities for new businesses than a mature, well-developed market. For example: mobile devices versus desktop computers.
- ❏ Customer characteristics and their buying habits – how will they find you? How can they be persuaded to choose your solution?
- ❏ Current and future competition – what are the choices now and how will they be different in the future?
- ❏ Test marketing – how do prospective customers respond to your pitch, price, packaging and promotional messages?

The most convincing market feedback, of course, is sales success. If you do not yet have that, then maybe you can get letters of intent, conditional orders or at least enthusiastic endorsements from prospective customers.

Once you have collected all that solid market research you can more confidently define your concept and your business strategy to approach your target customers.

WHICH BUSINESS MODEL?

After you have found the right market opportunity, the next important strategic decision is you choice of business model. Here are some of the alternatives to consider and the markets where they may be the best fit:

- ❑ Home based business, self-employed – personal service business
- ❑ Multi-level marketing business – importer/distributor of packaged consumer products
- ❑ Independent contractor – a trade or professional services
- ❑ Licensed agent – insurance, real estate, financial services
- ❑ Franchise – retail, hospitality, fast food, business services
- ❑ Independent corporation – local, national or global manufacturer, distributor or service provider
- ❑ Independent sole proprietor or multiple owner partnership – Retail, hospitality or food services, consumer services, and business-to-business services
- ❑ Entrepreneurial role within a large organisation or corporate environment
- ❑ Virtual business – Web, Internet or technology based business that has an online presence only

Your choices may be limited by your start-up resources; or may be obvious for the type of business that you want to be in. It may be appropriate to start with one type of business and evolve to another as your business grows – from a home office to an incorporated business or from a single location retailer to a national franchisor.

Now that you have defined and clarified the business opportunity and selected your start-up business model, the next step is to test the financial feasibility of your plan.

Is your idea ready for prime time as a profitable business or is it a bad idea that needs to be discarded in favour of a better plan?

6 Test Financial Feasibility

Can you make money with this idea?

Some initial financial feasibility tests will help to refine and develop your plan so that it leads you to build and grow a profitable business. The objective is to determine the level of sales required to reasonably ensure sustainable profitability.

You will need to use the data you have collected from the market research, make some initial assumptions about investment costs, revenue and expense, then test alternative scenarios to determine how to make your business profitable.

Net Profit at Breakeven is Zero.

Above the breakeven level of sales your business becomes profitable. Below breakeven you are losing money.

Start with this list of requirements to determine breakeven sales levels and compare them to your forecasts.

1. Forecast the Sales per Month that you expect after the first year in Units and in Revenue Dollars.

2. Determine the average price and average cost per unit. If you have a mix of products or services, use the forecast total monthly sales revenue and the corresponding monthly cost of those sales.

3. Calculate Average Gross Profit Margin, in three ways:

    1) Dollar Gross Margin per Unit = $ Price/unit - $ Cost/unit

2) Percent Gross Margin per Unit =$ Gross Margin per unit ÷ $ Price per unit

3) Average Gross Margin Percent = Dollars in Gross Margin per month ÷ Dollars in Sales per month

4. Estimate Fixed Expense per month including cost of Administration, Overhead, Marketing and Sales expense, but not including those items already in the variable cost of sales above.

Now you have everything you need to calculate the breakeven level of sales and test whether your forecast sales revenue will be profitable.

The following steps and examples below will guide you through the process. Remember "Breakeven" is that level of sales that will deliver just enough gross profit to cover the fixed monthly expenses of the business.

CALCULATE BREAKEVEN USING THESE FORMULAS:

❏ Breakeven Unit Sales = Fixed Expense ÷ Dollars Gross Margin per Unit

❏ Breakeven Sales Revenue = Monthly Fixed Expense ÷ Average Percent Gross Margin

For example:

❏ Average selling price is $12.00 for the products sold; the average cost is $9.00.

❏ Therefore, Average Gross Profit Margin = $3.00 per Unit or 25% of Sales (i.e. $3 ÷ $12 = 25%)

❏ Monthly fixed operating cost is $24,000/mo. (Fixed costs include: salaries, rent, utilities, insurance, interest, marketing, etc. – everything payable monthly regardless of the level of sales.)

❑ **Calculated Breakeven Unit Sales:**
= Fixed expense of $24,000/month ÷ $3 per unit = 8000
Units/month (i.e. @$12 each, sales of $96,000/month)

❑ **Calculated Breakeven Sales Revenue:**
= Fixed expense of $24,000/month ÷ 25% = $96,000 Sales/
month
(Confirming the unit sales calculation.)

❑ **Profit is zero at sales of $96,000/month:**
= ($96,000 Sales x 25% Gross Margin) – ($24,000/month
Fixed Costs)= $24,000 profit margin - $24,000 fixed costs =
$0 profit

The conclusion, therefore, is that the business will only be profitable above sales of $96,000 per month, given the 25% profit margin and $24,000/month in fixed costs.

Two additional considerations to be included in your feasibility tests to ensure long-term profitability and positive cash flow for your business:

❑ **Recovery of start-up costs**

❑ **Cash flow breakeven**

1. RECOVERY OF START-UP COSTS

Assume the investment cost to start this business is $180,000, which you want to pay back (amortize) over five years (60 months).

This requirement adds $3000 per month in depreciation allowance (i.e. $180,000 ÷ 60 months). That additional amount should be considered to determine what level of sales will provide for recovery of the total costs: the initial investment plus the monthly fixed operating costs.

In this example:

- ❏ Monthly Investment Recovery Cost = $24,000 in fixed expenses including loan interest payments, plus the $3000/month in capital repayment.
- ❏ Revised Breakeven = ($24,000 + $3000) ÷ $3 Gross Margin/unit = 9000 Units. ($108,000 per month at $12 per unit)
- ❏ Alternatively, using Percent Gross Margin: Breakeven = ($24,000 + $3000) ÷ 25%GM = $108,000/mo. (same as above)

2. CASH FLOW BREAKEVEN

Borrowing to finance the investment of $180,000 may require loan capital payments of $6000 per month, which is higher than your depreciation allowance and is in addition to the monthly interest charges already included in the fixed operating costs.

This will affect your cash flow breakeven which is also important to ensure that your financing plan is adequate.

Calculating Cash Flow Breakeven:

- ❏ Monthly Cash Cost = $24,000 including loan interest payments, plus the $6000 cash required in loan capital payments instead of the $3000 in non-cash amortization = $30,000.
- ❏ Cash Flow Breakeven = $30,000 ÷ $3 Gross Margin/unit = 10,000 units. ($120,000 Sales at $12 per unit)

These breakeven calculations provide appropriate benchmarks for you to assess the feasibility of your business under the initial assumptions for costs and revenues.

Now compare these breakeven sales levels to your sales forecasts to determine profitability:

FORECAST SALES > BREAKEVEN = PROFIT$$$!

As long as your forecast sales are greater than the breakeven sales level, your business will be profitable.

If your forecasts do <u>not</u> lead to profitability, then you need to revise, or abandon, the plan. Do not simply increase your forecasts by raising the unit sales or the selling prices, unless you can support the revisions with new market research data or changes in marketing and sales strategies.

If revised sales forecasts are not appropriate then perhaps profitability can be achieved by reducing the product costs to increase gross profit margins or by lowering the fixed monthly operating expenses. Either or both reductions in costs will lower the breakeven point and improve profitability at the forecast level of sales.

Once you have completed the feasibility tests and arrived at reasonable assumptions for revenue and costs that deliver profitability, you are ready to get started on documenting a detailed business plan. You have now confirmed the market opportunity, your personal capabilities and the approach that will turn it into a profitable business. The first recycling of your plan is done.

The next steps require more strategic decisions to develop your operating plans and financial projections in more detail.

→ 7 ⟩ Stop Daydreaming, Get Started

Choose a business model that fits

Decisions need to be made on the choices of business model, legal structure and start-up strategy which will be best for your business. At this point you have confirmed the market opportunity, defined your business concept and approach to the market and you have tested financial feasibility.

These are the next decisions to be made:
- ❏ Legal structure
  - Sole proprietorship, partnership, or corporation?

- ❏ Start-up process
  - Build from zero?
  - Buy an existing business?
  - Rent a business (i.e. "buy" a franchise), or
  - Assume leadership of a family business.

Your choice to buy, build, rent or inherit will depend on the realistic options available to you, your personal preferences, and the business concept that you plan to pursue.

Here are some of the issues to consider in making the right decision and getting started with the right business model and legal structure.

A sole proprietorship may be the best choice for a self-employed entrepreneur in a trade or profession where the business is essentially providing an alternative source of personal income. If you are "working for yourself" no formal legal structure is required; revenue and expense are simply included on your personal tax return under Business Income. It is a simple and low cost structure to start, or discontinue if necessary. Financial statements for the business will be required, but you can probably prepare them yourself and you may not require an accountant to prepare your tax returns.

The *disadvantages* are that you have less flexibility in splitting business and personal income, both the timing and the amounts, and *you remain personally responsible* for any business liabilities.

This may be the biggest risk — you are not protected from the liabilities that you incur through the business. They will be yours personally and your personal assets may be at risk unless you purchase liability insurance or you have limited liability agreements with everyone who does business with you. Both of those arrangements may be good ideas anyway, if they are practical and affordable.

A sole proprietorship is also less attractive to potential employees, suppliers, lenders or investors for them to do business with you. It is seen as having limited potential and perhaps less commitment from the owner than an incorporated business. So, in a sole proprietorship you are pretty much on your own to finance and operate the business.

A business partnership may be the right structure if you want to share management responsibilities and add skills, knowledge and experience beyond your own. In a partnership of any kind, care should be taken to have clear, documented legal agreements that define your shared responsibilities and your shared participation in profits, assets and liabilities.

In some regulated professions or industries, you may not be allowed to incorporate and only a personally registered business or partnership is acceptable. Check with the regulatory authorities and your legal advisors to be sure that you are meeting the industry requirements.

For most businesses, I recommend **incorporation**.

An incorporated business is a strong indication to all observers of your serious long-term commitment to the business and it makes the very important legal distinction between the business and its owners and shareholders.

The corporation is recognized as a legal entity that has rights, obligations and liabilities that are separate from those of the shareholders whose liability is limited to their investment in the business.

The corporation is taxed separately, and differently, from its shareholder owners. Ownership and management are clearly separated so that ownership can be sold or transferred without necessarily affecting the management team or operation of the business.

An incorporated business has the following particular advantages over other legal forms of business structure:

❑ Clear separation of owner and management roles and responsibilities
❑ More attractive to other participants, such as lenders, investors, employees, customers and strategic partners
❑ Easy transfer or sale of ownership
❑ An indefinite life span, separate from the founders and owners
❑ Unlimited potential to grow and to be financed by additional shareholders, including the public.

There are, however, some disadvantages and additional costs associated with incorporation that must be recognized.

Incorporation is more expensive and complex than the other legal business structures to set up and will also create future obligations for annual reporting. You may require professional services from lawyers and accountants to meet all those obligations. The fees will increase with the size and complexity of the business from less than $1000 up to several tens of thousands of dollars per year. Choose your professionals early in the process and try to ensure that they meet your needs and budget limits to start, but can also grow with you and support your long term plans.

The incorporated business will be required to pay corporate income taxes in addition to any taxes on income to the shareholders, effectively increasing the total tax paid by the business owners on their personal and business income. Rates and regulations will depend on the jurisdiction where your business operates.

All these additional costs and complexities need to be weighed against the relative advantage of operating an incorporated business compared to the alternatives of a sole proprietorship or a business partnership.

STRATEGIC CHOICES FOR GETTING STARTED

Most business plans start from zero and build an idea into a profitable growing business. This Guide is primarily designed for those start-up businesses, but it can be used for business planning at any stage of the business life cycle.

For new entrepreneurs, the primary alternatives to consider for getting into a business are: **build, buy, rent, or inherit.**

It may be difficult to arrange to inherit a business if you are not already in the family, but you can more easily arrange one of the other start-up strategies to buy an existing business or "rent" one by buying into a franchised business instead of building from zero. Either of those options may reduce the unknowns and the risks associated with a start-up, but there are other important offsetting considerations.

Buying a Business

The advantages of buying an existing business are obvious:
❑ An existing entity with established markets, customers, employees, suppliers, and facilities

- ❏ The company, its products and brands are known in the market
- ❏ Added value of assets in operating condition, plus the intangibles of "goodwill"
- ❏ Easier to assess the opportunities for improvement and growth

Buying a business, however, also requires careful consideration of some particular risks:

- ❏ Reliability of reported financial results
- ❏ Unreported income or expenses from "cash" deals
- ❏ Mixture of personal and business, income and expense
- ❏ Dependence on a few customers or suppliers
- ❏ Dependence on key employees
- ❏ Continuity of management style, corporate culture and employee loyalty
- ❏ Quality of facilities and equipment
- ❏ Financial obligations, leases and contracts
- ❏ Customer and employee relations - legal issues
- ❏ Competitive threats
- ❏ Protection of products, trademarks, brand names, sales territories
- ❏ Potential liabilities from product failures, warranties and recalls or refunds.
- ❏ Regulatory issues – taxes, legal, environmental, social responsibility, national and local

Any one of these risks may be significant enough to cause you to walk away from acquiring the business.

Note, however, that many of the risks can be eliminated if you are able to buy only the assets that are of interest to you. Unfortunately, the owners may not be interested in having you strip out the good assets as that severely reduces the remaining value of their equity and on an asset sale they lose the preferred tax treatment that only applies to the sale of owner equity.

Franchised Business

Buying into a business franchise has similar advantages and disadvantages that must be considered:

- ❏ Nature and quality of the business
- ❏ Value of the brand name
- ❏ Franchisor support and their proven business model
- ❏ Franchise costs and additional investment costs

Most importantly, will owning a franchise meet your objectives for independence and success as an entrepreneur? Will you be acting only as a passive investor or more like an employee-manager for the franchisor?

These alternative business models and methods to start your business require careful consideration and analysis before you launch.

Real Life Story: "Too many choices. I'll take that one."

Looking over all the choices and decisions to be made before starting your new business, it can be tempting to skip all the hard work of research and analysis and just get on with it. Take the easy and obvious choice in front of you – join the family business, take that franchise offer, or accept the promotion with your current employer.

But easy and obvious does not mean it's the right decision. Starting a business means accepting the risk of the unknown and having confidence that you will find a way to succeed. You will never know if it's a bad idea or a missed opportunity until you push forward against the odds, the critics and your own self-doubt.

For example:

"I hired a new General Manager to replace me so I could retire from my business. It didn't work out, so I got my two kids to run it for me instead."

It was a bad decision. For him and his kids and for the business. He was in continual conflict with his son, who wasn't interested in the company or the job. His daughter was committed to her father and the business, but did not have the education or experience to manage alone. The business was in rapid decline.

Accepting the easy and obvious was the wrong choice. All three of them should have made other decisions to ensure continuity of the business and to realize their separate personal ambitions to retire or pursue other career paths.

Take charge of your future. Make better choices.

Once you have made the initial decisions — choosing the opportunity and your business model and legal structure and answering all the other start-up questions, you are ready to begin preparing the final business plan documents and financial projections.

My recommended business plan outline and checklist of the required contents are described in the next chapter.

Recommended Business Plan Outline and Checklist

8

What should be in your Business Plan?

The following sections provide a complete outline and checklist of the required contents for a successful Business Plan.

These recommendations describe the layout and content for presentation of your Business Plan. Each section lists what should be included to complete each part of your plan. You can choose your own style and format, but complete all the sections required in order to get the results you want from both the process and the document.

Be convincing, but be concise.

Nobody wants to waste their time reading a long rambling presentation that does not quickly get to the point. Typically, I recommend that your plan should be not more than fifteen to twenty pages, including three to five pages of financial projections with more detail and supporting documentation placed in the Appendices.

It is also important to provide a brief Executive Summary (see below) and to be able to deliver an "Elevator Pitch". That's the 30-second to 2-minute version of your plan that you can deliver to the bank CEO when you catch him (or her) in the elevator on the way to the executive suite and want to persuade him (or her) to invest in your business.

In the following sections I describe the required contents and the recommended sequence for presentation. You can of course be creative and do it differently, but in my experience that is where you start to mess up the message. Don't make that mistake.

Keep it simple. Answer all the questions you can and don't try to bluff or B.S. your way through any of them. Recognize where your plan is weak and deal with it.

TITLE PAGE

Aside from making a good first impression by presenting your business plan in a colorful glossy binder, the title page should include the name of the company, revision date, statement of purpose, prepared by whom for whom and a copy control number.

This page should also include any disclaimers (i.e. no guarantee of the forecast results, it's best efforts only) and provide for sign-off by the reader on your terms for confidentiality, non-disclosure, non-conflict of interest and non-compete.

All of this helps to demonstrate that you are serious and that you are a disciplined and detail-oriented manager. It's important to the reader!

PURPOSE

Include a short description of the purpose of the document on the title page or in an introductory cover note.

What are your objectives in submitting this Business Plan for review? Who is reading it and what do you expect from them? Is it meant to attract financing, key executives, first customers or strategic partners? Is it only for internal use to document the corporate strategy, action plan, financial objectives and timetable?

CONTENTS AND CHECKLIST:

The following table of contents ensures that that you will meet all of the requirements, but again you can rearrange or consolidate sections, if you are convinced that it improves the presentation and personalization of your Business Plan.

Table of Contents

1. Executive summary

2. Concept and business opportunity

3. Mission, Vision, Values

4. Market Analysis

5. Competition

6. Strategic Objectives and Action Plan

7. Management Team and Organization Plan

8. Products and Services

9. Marketing and Sales Plan

10. Operations Plan

11. Risk analysis

12. Financial plan

13. Conclusion

14. Appendices

The requirements for each of these sections are described below.

1. Executive Summary
This is a maximum of two to three pages, written last as a stand-alone summary document. (You may have chosen to do a draft of the executive summary to use as your initial business plan outline, but it should be revised as a final step.)

The executive summary may be offered for review prior to full disclosure of the business plan. It should be the primary "pitch" document that convinces the reader to go further, or not.

Include:
- ❏ Market opportunity
- ❏ Business concept, strategic plan and objectives
- ❏ Current status relative to the market opportunity
- ❏ Key success factors, risks, expected results

❏ Financial situation and needs
❏ Request for participation or financing

2. Concept and Business Opportunity

Expand on the brief Executive Summary to describe the customer needs being addressed, how your approach is different and why it is likely to succeed.

Include:
❏ Market need, customer demand and the current solutions available
❏ Business concept and business model or financial structure
❏ Product or service differentiation
❏ Initial market feedback to confirm likely success

3. Mission, Vision, Values Statement

Generate missionaries! Why should others join your cause – to have fun, make money, or make a difference? Where, how, for whom?

Include:
❏ Clear, attractive objectives – what you want to be and when
❏ Statement of values and priorities for management
❏ Key milestones and timetable for achieving them

4. Market Analysis

Provide relevant, pertinent information to demonstrate your knowledge and competence in this industry.

Include:
❏ The overall market, recent changes
❏ Market segments that are attractive to you
❏ Target market niche and the type of customers targeted
❏ Customer characteristics and the factors that will make them buyers
❏ Buying and selling process and where you will fit into it

5. Competition

Demonstrate an awareness of specific competitors and confirm your ability to compete successfully. Do <u>not</u> suggest that you have no competition. Your prospective customers always have choices, including ignoring you.

Include:

- ❏ Industry overview, recent trends
- ❏ Nature of competition, from inside and outside the industry
- ❏ Primary competitors – brief descriptions, compared to your concept
- ❏ Competitive products and services, relative pricing, advantages and disadvantages compared to your offering
- ❏ Competitive opportunities and their limits due to protection by patents, copyrights, other barriers to entry (theirs and yours)
- ❏ Potential competitive response — their ability to out-market, underprice, imitate or copy you.

6. Strategic Plan

Describe your starting point, direction, objectives and the plan to get there.

Include:

- ❏ Company history, background and current status
- ❏ Describe experience and resources available to you
- ❏ Describe key competitive strengths and current weaknesses
- ❏ Strategies to leverage your strengths and reduce your weaknesses
- ❏ Action Plan: Provide the details of the key action steps in each area — financial, organizational, operations, sales and marketing — with planned deliverables and dates for each step.

7. Management Team and Organisation Plan

This is often the most important factor in determining your success and in attracting additional staff and financing. Confidence in your business plan is based on the people responsible for it. Emphasize your current experience and competencies and your plan to fill in the gaps.

Include:
- ❏ Owner/management team, plus advisors, supporters
- ❏ Key personnel – experience and credentials
- ❏ Staffing plan and organizational structure

8. Products and Services

Consider the reader's familiarity with the industry and avoid or explain technical jargon. Present your offering relative to the market and to what is available from current suppliers.

Include:
- ❏ Product or service descriptions
- ❏ Positioning of the products and services relative to alternatives
- ❏ Competitive evaluation of products and services
- ❏ Future plans for products and services

9. Marketing and Sales Plan

Marketing and sales effectiveness are essential to any successful business and must be well presented in your plan. They are too often neglected by business owners with strong professional, technical, or operations backgrounds.

Don't ever think or say out loud, "The product will sell itself."

Prepare a marketing and sales plan that will be practical, affordable and effective.

Include:
- ❏ Marketing strategy, positioning, presentation
- ❏ Confirm plans to use advertising, promotions/incentives, publicity, public relations, direct mail, trade shows, or industry events
- ❏ Describe online initiatives for Web marketing and sales

BUSINESS PLAN OUTLINE AND CHECKLIST

❏ Sales plan and tactics – use of direct sales staff, agents, distributors or retail channels

10. Operations Plan

Describe the important issues and factors that will affect manufacturing and delivery of your products or services and the follow-up customer service and support. Define the relevant initial investments required and the ongoing operating costs.

Include:
❏ Description of the facilities and equipment required
❏ Processes for product or service delivery
❏ Customer service and support – policy and plans
❏ Staffing, compensation and benefit plans

11. Risk Analysis

This is the section that deals with all the contingency plans. What can go wrong; what will you do about it?

How can you prevent it or protect yourself? The risks may be predictable, but are probably not avoidable.

Include:
❏ Market factors outside management control: economic cycles, interest rates, currency exchange rates, government regulations, trade restrictions
❏ Business risks within management control: key customer and supplier dependence, labor availability, staff turnover, new competitors, new technology and changing demand
❏ Confirm contracts and legal protection, insurance plans

12. Financial Plan

In this section, convert all the preceding words into numbers; preferably with details of the next year by month, then the following three-to-five years of annual forecast results.

Include:
- ❏ Summary of business and financial assumptions in the forecasts
- ❏ Financial history to date, if applicable
- ❏ Starting Balance Sheet showing initial start-up costs and required financing
- ❏ Forecast sales revenue and gross margins
- ❏ Forecast fixed and variable expenses
- ❏ Profit and Loss Projections
- ❏ Cash Flow Projections
- ❏ Balance Sheet Projections
- ❏ Target performance benchmarks and financial ratios
- ❏ An estimate of the future value of equity

You may choose to show your detailed financial projections in the appendices and extract only summary financial results for the main document. That will help to focus the reader on key numbers instead of getting lost in the details before concluding whether to proceed or not.

You can also provide a summary of expected financial results with a graphic presentation, as in this example:

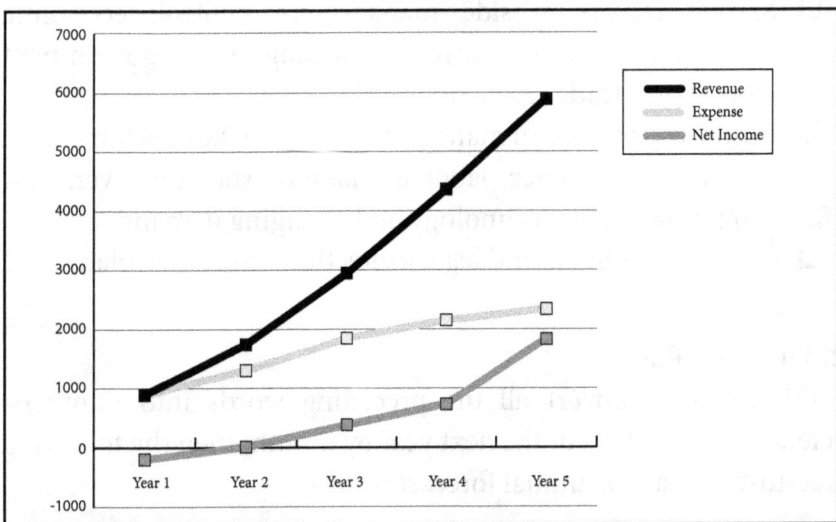

Samples of financial projections are shown with the example Business Plans provided in the Appendix to this Guide.

13. Conclusion

This is the final section where you ask for what you want.

Reiterate the purpose of the Business Plan and confirm what you expect from the reader. Make it clear what you are asking for and when you expect an answer. Keep it confident and enthusiastic.

Appendices to the Business plan

The Appendices are an opportunity to prove that you have done your homework and that all your assumptions and forecasts are well-supported. This is also the place to add some personalization and realism to the Business Plan.

In addition to the detailed financial projections, include:

- ❏ sample marketing materials
- ❏ product photos, drawings, specifications
- ❏ biographies and photos of key executives
- ❏ facility and equipment plans and descriptions
- ❏ cost estimates or supplier quotations
- ❏ press releases, customer testimonials or letters of intent
- ❏ relevant market research documents or published articles that support your analysis

And that completes your Business Plan!

Follow these guidelines to ensure that you have considered all the issues and that you can defend your strategies and action plans against all inquisitors. You will then have a Business Plan that is most likely to get you the response that you want from those that review it. **Maybe even the financing.**

Real Life Story: "The answer is still NO!"

This is another true story and, I'm sorry, it's not very encouraging. In spite of everything I have just explained about preparing a great Business Plan, you still may not get the financing you want.

In the early 2000's during the infamous dot.com bubble, my partner and I decided to launch an e-commerce venture that was essentially a virtual distribution business for computer products. We consolidated product information from various sources in a database and then developed an online catalogue application for computer retailers to shop for all the products showing the comparative pricing from alternative sources. We also offered retailers a customized storefront where they could present the same products to their customers and accept orders. It may sound pretty boring now, but this was in the early days of e-commerce and online shopping.

We got rave reviews from the computer distributors and retailers, "Wow, how do you do that?" Lots of users and sponsors signed up. But it was going to be costly to develop and support and we were not generating much revenue – so it was time to prepare a business plan and get the million dollar financing we needed to conquer the world.

We did the research and prepared the documents and financial projections to support a multi-million dollar valuation and started knocking on doors. Again we got rave reviews. "Great product, great Business Plan, etc., etc."

Everything looked good for us: two experienced entrepreneurs with prior successes in the same industry; a proven business model with early customers in place; a realistic plan to build and grow the business; and reasonable projections to deliver a high return on investment.

But the answer was still, "NO!"

Everyone had a different reason not to invest in us, but they all concluded with "Good luck, but goodbye."

So we finally concluded ourselves that it was time to let it go and cut our losses. Like many dot.coms and other high tech start-ups with great credentials and exciting potential, we wound up the business and went back to pursuing other career and business options.

It may happen to you. Don't be discouraged.

It's just time to accept the lessons learned and come up with a new plan. You may not have to change your goals, just your plan for getting there.

Get the Financing You Need

What are the most likely sources?
What do they want to see?

With your Business Plan completed, you will now be ready to approach sources of financing. There are many alternatives available, but you will probably go through them in the following order:

- ❏ Personal investment – your own cold cash
- ❏ "Sweat equity" – personal time and effort, unpaid
- ❏ "Love money" — from willing friends, family and fools
- ❏ Bank financing — term loans, lines of credit, mortgages on fixed assets
- ❏ Angel investors – personal investors with the added value of knowledge and contacts
- ❏ Government funding, special loans, grants or subsidies
- ❏ Venture capital, private equity financing
- ❏ An IPO – Initial Public Offering of shares in the business

Each of these sources will need a slightly different approach to appeal to their specific interests and concerns, but a well prepared business plan will be essential in persuading them to participate.

Very Important Note

Before you use the business plan to request financing, be sure you can meet the one key requirement that is the most common reason for failing to get additional financing.

**Put enough of your own cash at risk before trying
to persuade other people to hand over theirs.**

Demonstrate your confidence and commitment, then show how much total financing you expect to require before the business becomes cash flow positive and starts to contribute to financing itself. Different sources may step in to participate as you reach different milestones and require additional funds to continue your growth.

Eventually, however, every investor wants their money back with a reasonable return on the investment in line with the risks that were accepted when they chose to participate. You will have to meet those expectations.

Real Life Stories: "Don't say that out loud."

When you are finally sitting down with the banker or potential investor and reviewing your impressive and irresistible business plan, please be careful what you say out loud. Try to stick to the script in your pitch and business plan.

These are not your new best friends, regardless of how friendly and helpful they seem. Remember they are there to avoid any risk of losing their funds and to ensure they will make money in your business. They are there to support their career plans, not your business plan. Don't ever embarrass them or cause them to regret financing you. You need to be building their confidence in the plan and your ability to deliver. I have had some clients blurt out admissions that did not help their cause with the bankers, investors or potential partners they were meeting.

Some real life examples:

> "We don't have any more money to put in. Our mortgage loan is already at the maximum."

> "I didn't really want to work with my wife on this project, but I had a nervous breakdown and lost my job. It's hard to find anything else."

> "The prototype is not working yet, but I'm sure we'll get it right and have our first order soon."

> "We didn't do much research, but this is obviously a multi-billion dollar market, so we only need 0.002 percent market share to meet our sales projections. And the product sells itself."

> "I don't know where those numbers came from."

Try to be more discrete when you're forced to admit some of the deficencies in your plan. Recognize the potential problems, questions and concerns and be ready to handle them. Getting additional financing will require more than a well-documented business plan to persuade new investors to join you. You will need to be an effective spokesperson and negotiator.

When you succeed in getting sufficient financing to launch your business, you can then turn your attention to the challenges of managing it. That is the subject of the next chapter.

10

The Entrepreneur's Challenge

Strategic Leadership and Management Effectiveness

Once you have your business started, the real challenge will be to successfully run a profitable and growing business. There are many opportunities to make mistakes and to stumble into unexpected problems.

From my experience, confirmed by other entrepreneurs, it's OK to occasionally fail and to make mistakes; as long as they are small and recognized early.

It's all part of the learning experience to get better. But there are some big mistakes that can kill your business.

Real Life Stories: The Seven Biggest Mistakes

A few years ago, I had a request was to do a presentation to a group of entrepreneurs, including professionals and their clients, at a networking breakfast.

The suggested topic was, "Tell us how to avoid the mistakes that entrepreneurs make." The next question was "What are the most common mistakes?" and "How many should we cover."

So we did a survey of entrepreneurs and their advisors and received a long list with many creative descriptions of the "biggest" or the "most serious." There were stories to go with every one of them, too many to include in this brief guide to business plans. I organised and consolidated around seven common themes and then developed recommendations on how to avoid the biggest mistakes.

Following is my latest version of the continuously revised and updated list.

The Seven Biggest Mistakes that Entrepreneurs Make and How to Avoid Them

#1. Too Entrepreneurial

Certain characteristics of entrepreneurs are necessary for them to be successful. But if overdone they can lead to big mistakes. These include the tendency to be too opportunistic and not sufficiently selective and focused; to be too optimistic and miss or ignore the warning signs; to be too impatient and expect too much too soon.

Entrepreneurs usually have great confidence in their instincts and consequently rely on "gut feel". The mistake is to neglect or ignore market feedback and analysis. Being action-oriented, the tendency is to react and "fire" before the "ready, aim" phases are complete. Painful surprises can result.

Many successful entrepreneurs have achieved a lot based on their energy, charm, charisma, and persuasiveness, but then they get caught continuing to sell on personality and not delivering on performance. Clients start to notice that expectations are not being met.

Entrepreneurs are expected to be decisive and demonstrate "leadership". But both can be overdone – deciding too quickly and providing too much direction, so that input, initiative and creativity are stifled.

"Doing it my way" often means improvising and learning on the fly or sticking with what works until it stops working. The mistake is in neglecting to evolve and grow by continuously improving systems and installing the best practices and latest technologies.

All these mistakes can lead to serious consequences, as a result of being too entrepreneurial.

#2. Lack of Strategic Direction

Action-oriented entrepreneurs tend to get lost in the daily operating requirements and frequently ignore the original strategic plan and objectives. The owner-manager becomes pre-occupied with operating decisions and all the demands on his time from customers, suppliers and employees. The constant firefighting leaves little time for fire prevention.

This situation is worsened as the entrepreneur concludes that the best solution is "do-it-myself." Not delegating to staff and not using external expertise may seem like the least-cost solution, but probably misapplies the owner's time and expertise and does not lead to long-term solutions.

The entrepreneur may have good awareness of long-term strategic issues and had them in mind when the business was launched. But they are now neglected, and the original business plan (if there was one) is not reviewed, updated or shared.

Lack of consistent strategic direction may be the single Biggest Mistake that entrepreneurs make in running their businesses.

#3. Focused on Profit

Being focused on profit doesn't seem like a mistake. After all, isn't that the whole purpose of running a business?

No, actually. As I explain to students in their first Finance class, the primary financial objective of any business is *to build long-term sustainable business value.*

Many short-term profit-oriented decisions can hurt long-term value. The examples are many: reducing staff, cutting maintenance or marketing expenses; not upgrading systems and technology; accepting high credit risk or low margin customers to make the extra sale; avoiding regulatory requirements; ignoring environmental or quality issues.

Most entrepreneurs are very focused on managing the bottom line by monitoring their monthly sales, gross margins and expenses. They always know those numbers.

But they often neglect asset management, especially cash flow. The business may appear very profitable, but have constant cash flow challenges because of poor management of inventory and receivables, for example. Unfortunately, it is not as simple as: *"Collect Fast, Pay Slow."* And customer and supplier relationships can be at risk if cash flow issues force you to take that approach too aggressively.

Managing the Balance Sheet also requires good management of debt and balancing short-term and long-term needs with short-term and long-term sources of funds.

And the *Most Undervalued Asset* doesn't usually even appear on the Balance Sheet: *Human Resources.*

That leads to Biggest Mistake #4.

#4. Neglecting Key Relationships

The most important key relationship for any business is the one between management and staff. Management and employee communications are essential to business performance and often are not managed very well. Key employees need to be recognized and engaged. Mistakes made with key employees can jeopardize the whole business.

Similarly, don't make the mistake of being distracted by the most annoying and persistent customers. Your biggest customers are not likely the "squeakiest," just the most important. Don't let them be neglected.

Do you need to squeak more yourself? Do your major suppliers appreciate you enough? Fast growth and profitability may be coming from one or two key customers or suppliers which can lead to your over-dependence on them. And your success at connecting suppliers to customers may be convincing them both that they don't need you in the middle any more. Be wary.

Another key relationship not to be neglected: your bank. Is your bank a welcome and willing partner in your business? Remember "friends in need" have to be developed in advance.

#5. Poor Marketing and Sales Management

You know there is a problem brewing when you hear the entrepreneur explaining that "The product sells itself," or "Price is all that really matters," or "Our sales reps need to close better."

These are all symptoms of poor marketing and sales management. Usually the company is failing at both the strategic planning level and in the execution of effective marketing and sales programs.

Not only are opportunities for profitable growth being missed, but the company may be on the downward slide to out-of-business without a well-conceived marketing plan and effective sales management.

#6. "That was Easy, Let's Do It Again!"

Another common mistake that can have devastating consequences for the business is the over-confident entrepreneur who concludes, "That was easy, let's do it again!" So he or she leaps into new markets, new product lines, or even a new business or investment opportunity.

It's important to remember: Making money doesn't make you smarter. Do you really know what you did to succeed? Or what mistakes and risks you avoided? Was it good management or good luck?

Is now a good time to start something new? How much will the current business be affected by your new initiatives?

Many successful entrepreneurs have made the mistake of jumping into a new venture — merger, acquisition, restaurant franchise or real estate investment — and blown away the equity value they generated in their original business.

It's another big mistake to avoid.

#7. Distracted by Personal Issues

Personalities and personal issues can seriously affect business performance, regardless of whether it's the owner, management or staff. Sometimes they are recognized, but simply ignored until they become a problem. Sometimes personal distractions are a result of too much success — behaving like a rock star.

Family businesses have particular issues that may add risk and interfere with business success. Perceived favouritism and family matters at work can be distractions for everyone. Managing personalities and corporate culture are a particular challenge in family businesses.

That completes my list of the **Seven Biggest Mistakes that Entrepreneurs Make**:

1. Too Entrepreneurial
2. Lack of Strategic Direction
3. Focus on Profit
4. Neglecting Key Relationships
5. Poor Marketing and Sales
6. "Let's do it again!"
7. Personal Distractions

HOW TO AVOID THEM?
THE ANSWER IS: BALANCE!

Each of these mistakes is a result of the entrepreneur failing to achieve balance between the opposing demands on time, resources and priorities. Good choices and better decisions need to be made.

Avoiding these mistakes requires the entrepreneur to:

- ❏ Balance the Entrepreneurial Approach with Analytical Input

- ❏ Balance Strategic Vision with Management Effectiveness

- ❏ Add the Head and the Heart to the Gut Feel

❑ Manage for Long-term Value not just Short-term Profit

❑ Keep Personal Priorities in your Plan, but out of your Business

Managing to balance these issues will help you to grow and prosper in your business and avoid the Seven Biggest Mistakes that Entrepreneurs Make.

You can learn more about the mistakes and how to avoid them in Uncle Ralph's book sharing stories between entrepreneurs called, DON'T DO IT THE HARD WAY, also now available in a new 2020 Edition.

Avoid the mistakes!

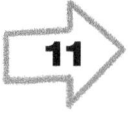

11

Package your Business for Sale

Looking good and ready to sell will maximize value.

Even if your business is not for sale, you should manage it every day like it will be for sale someday. Are you running your own business or just giving yourself a job? Real entrepreneurs always manage their business to maximize its value – for the current owners and for future buyers.

It may not be a short-term objective to exit your business, but it is always a wise management strategy to package your business as if it's for sale.

That means making it independent of you, the owner, and ensuring that the performance metrics are attractive and easily understood by outsiders. Meeting those two criteria will immediately make the business more valuable and also less demanding on you until you're ready to exit.

It essentially means looking at your business as a dispassionate investor instead of the emotionally attached owner. Step back and look at your business as it would appear to an outsider who is trying to put a value on it.

Remember that business value is based on only two things: Expected future income and the certainty or risk associated with achieving it.

The issues that affect the assessment of future income are:

❏ Strategy, competitive positioning and branding

❏ Product or service plans, pricing, quality and service

❏ Cost control — variable and fixed

❏ Asset management — cash, inventory, receivables, facilities and equipment

Performance tracking and planned improvements will require analysis of the financial ratios compared to your industry, specific competitors if possible, and checking trends over time. A future buyer, not to mention any banker or potential investor, will consider all these factors.

The issues that affect the assessment of risk and valuation of the business are:

- Reliability of financial statements
- Dependence on a few customers or suppliers
- Dependence on key employees, especially the owner or family members
- Quality of management, employee relations
- Strength of customer and supplier relationships
- Competitive threats
- Condition of facilities and equipment
- Financial obligations, loans and leases
- Protection of product design, intellectual property, trademarks, brand names, territories
- Potential liabilities — product failures, warranty claims, recalls
- Regulatory issues — taxes, legal, environmental

You can enhance the value of your business simply by working on increasing the annual net income and reducing the uncertainty.

That means making the business more profitable, more stable and less dependent on you. It probably means installing a management team that can deliver the results without your direct involvement. That's a worthy objective anyway as it will make the business easier for you to exit at some point and will reduce the demands on you in the short term.

Packaging your business for sale helps you immediately to make it a better business; both more valuable and easier to manage.

Real Life Story: "It's a Fixer-Upper"

They say in selling real estate that the three most important factors are: location, location, location. In selling your business, they are: timing, timing, timing.

I was working with a client that had been manufacturing industrial supply products for almost forty years. The two owner-managers were in their seventies and thinking they should start working on their retirement plans and maybe find new owners to take over the business. Sales revenue had been stable with little growth over the past few years and profitability had been acceptable to the two current owners.

However, if they were going to sell the business and retire, then they wanted a big cash payout from the sale to bump up their retirement funds. That led to their expectations for a higher price than could be justified by their historical financial results.

They then made two bad decisions to try and achieve the business valuation they wanted.

They persuaded themselves that, "We're sure new owners can do even better than we've been doing," and "Let's wait until after we've had a really good year before we sell. Maybe next year."

Big mistakes.

First, new owners are never going to pay for value that they can deliver that the current owners could not. Second, a really good year may not come soon enough. The next year was a very bad year, due to circumstances beyond the control of the owners. So their retirement plans were put on hold, indefinitely.

Lesson learned?

Always build and manage your business for an early exit. Then it will be ready to sell at the best possible value, anytime. You may not get to choose the perfect timing. It may be an unexpected opportunity or an unexpected end.

Be prepared for both.

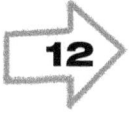

12 ▷ **Price it Right**

Look at it like a buyer, not the owner

If you are managing as an owner-entrepreneur then you should be focused on maximizing the value of your business. That means understanding what determines the price. Not your ego-inflated value of the business, but the price that a dispassionate investor or buyer would put on it.

In establishing the value of your business, some basic principles must be understood:

1. The value to the owner is unique to that individual. Ego may artificially inflate the price, but more importantly the roles and relationships established by the owner may change drastically with his or her departure, and thereby affect the price.

2. Value is always determined by an evaluation of the future income relative to the uncertainty or risks associated with obtaining the expected income.

   Regardless of the valuation method (P/E multiple, payback period, or discounted cash flow, described below), the forecast future income stream has to be credible and the known risks have to be reduced to get the best possible valuation.

3. Current owners tolerate more risk, uncertainty and fuzzy unknowns than new owners or investors. You may be OK with the fact that you're dependent on one key supplier who happens to be an old high school buddy; or that you have no signed lease, but the landlord is your favourite uncle; or that your best sales rep is also your son and he's hoping to be president soon.

Prospective buyers will be much less enthusiastic about these issues, unless they are all resolved to their satisfaction in advance of making any offer to purchase or invest.

4. Different buyers will accept different prices, terms and conditions.

   Their business valuations and purchase offers will usually be in a limited range: whether it's from the passive investor looking for a reasonable return with reasonable risk; or the active owner-manager who sees the potential to do better than you under his own management; or from the strategic investor who sees potentially higher returns in buying a competitor, supplier or customer and merging it with an existing business to increase revenues, reduce shared expenses and substantially increase profit.

   Your potential selling price will depend on the perceived value seen by each of these different buyers.

Several different valuation methodologies may be used by buyers and sellers. It is usually a good idea to test different approaches to see what values they yield and then select a selling price that can be reasonably supported by any method of valuation.

P/E Multiple

The price/earnings multiple is a well-recognized valuation method and widely reported for public companies. Current price per share divided by annual earnings per share is a simple concept and a simple calculation. Unfortunately, it is not always very useful, since the selling price today is more likely based on the expectation of future earnings, not prior years' earnings.

For example, Google's share price (GOOGL) on December 31st, 2019 was U.S. $1339.39 with the previous twelve months' earnings at $45.97 which yields a P/E multiple of 29.1 times. If we use the analysts' consensus estimate for future earnings of $51.88 per share, then the P/E multiple at that price would be a more "reasonable" 25.8 times. Google's high P/E multiple is based on analysts' expectations of continuing growth and profitability compared to the less exciting stocks, like TD Bank for example.

TD Bank shares (TD) were priced at U.S. $56.13 on December 31st, 2019 with the previous twelve months' earnings at $4.81 for a P/E multiple of only 11.7 times. Using the analysts' consensus estimate for future earnings of $6.88 per share, then the P/E multiple would be only 8.16 compared to the industry average of 13.3. You might conclude, therefore, that TD Bank is a good buy at that price and P/E multiple.

What is the P/E multiple for your company?

Typically, small owner-managed businesses can support a P/E multiple ranging from 2 to 5 times. It will be higher if earnings are stable and growing and not dependent on the current owner. The P/E multiple will be lower if future earnings are uncertain and very dependent on the current owner.

The buyer will usually look at operating income, often referred to as EBITDA (Earnings before Interest, Taxes, Depreciation and Amortization), to determine profitability before financing, taxes and capital costs. That means a selling price of $300,000 on your $100,000 per year operating income, if you agree on a P/E multiple of 3 times.

Payback Period

Some buyers will insist on looking only at net cash flow and the payback period to recover their full investment before arriving at a price. They will determine how long it takes to get their investment back and will likely have a minimum payback period, depending on the perceived risk, ranging from three to five years.

For example, if their requirement is a three year payback and your average annual net cash flow is $100,000, they will not offer more than $300,000 to buy your business.

Discounted Cash Flow

Other investors will take the financial analysts approach of calculating discounted Net Present Value (NPV) or the Return on Investment (ROI). Again the future net cash flows must be forecast for at least five years to arrive at a valuation. The buyer will then discount future cash flow at the required rate of return, typically 15% to 20%, or calculate the expected ROI compared to their required rate of return. For example, the $100,000 per year net cash flow on a $500,000 investment provides a 20% annual return on the investment. If you insist on a purchase price of $750,000, then the buyer's expected rate of return (ROI) will fall to 13.3%.

By using this method and agreeing on an acceptable rate of return, the buyers and sellers may be able negotiate a mutually acceptable price.

Using any of these methods will give you a range of valuations under various forecast scenarios to establish your own best estimate of a fair selling price.

Now you have a basis for comparison to value your business over time. It will be useful for starting negotiations with any prospective investor or buyer and may also help in a shareholder buy-sell agreement or succession plan when you are ready to exit.

Knowing the value of your business is a key performance measure that you should be tracking regularly. The day you need to know should not be the first time you calculate it.

Real Life Story: "It's worth how much?"

Many entrepreneurs ask the question, "What is my business worth?"

I usually recommend that a simple estimate of the value be included in the financial projections for every Business Plan. The principles of business valuation are widely accepted and the math is quite simple. But the real value is established only when a buyer and seller actually agree on a price. And that depends a lot on the particular buyer and seller, their current circumstances and their objectives, as illustrated by this story.

A former client with a well-established technology consulting business in Montreal called me a few years ago to give him my assessment of the value of his business. So I did my homework.

He had over twenty years of consistent profitability, a good reputation in the industry, some proprietary software products and major international corporate accounts. All that helped the valuation multiples and led me to estimate a value of $3 million to $3.5 million for his business. He was the sole shareholder.

He agreed that my valuation seemed reasonable. Then he said, "But I already have an offer for six million dollars."

"What!?"

So he explained that he had received an offer from a big European competitor in the same industry that wanted to acquire his business for six million dollars. However, he then discovered that once they owned it they planned to shut it down and move the operations into their North American offices in Cleveland.

That's when he said, "No thanks," at any price. Instead he proceeded with a plan to transfer equity to his key employees (at my valuation) to ensure their loyalty (which should have been assured by his declining to cash out and kiss them goodbye).

The business continues to grow and prosper in Montreal.

13 ▷ Some Final Words on Business Plans

RE-WRITE FOR EVERY READER

Your plan needs to be written differently for different readers and different purposes. Not a substantially different plan obviously, just different emphasis and focus on what the particular reader will want to know and what you want from them.

Edit your business plan accordingly for each reader. It is even more impressive if you personalize the cover page for each new audience.

Prior to approaching banks or financial institutions, you should visit their websites to find out what they're really looking for in their preferred business plan – content and presentation. Verify if they have a particular business plan template or application form that is required. You may discover that up to a certain loan amount, say $100,000, they only accept applications online (If they clearly want to avoid wasting their time on small business clients, you may decide to do the same and look for another bank.)

You may also discover that your personal financial statements and net worth are at least as important as your business plan. So get those in order before you attach them to your application for funding.

Some readers of your plan may be more focused on your credentials and experience; others on your marketing and sales plans to support the revenue forecasts; others on the technical specifications of your product. Cater to their interests.

Submission of your Executive Summary first will help you not only gauge their interest, but also determine which questions they will be seeking answers to.

THERE IS NEVER A FINAL VERSION

Your Business Plan is a working document that you should refer to regularly and review and revise annually. It was never intended for outsiders only or for one-time use only.

Of particular value for ongoing management of the business will be the definition of your financial goals, performance measures and the timetable and budgets in your strategic action plan.

Continuing to monitor your progress against the plan is absolutely the best way to keep on track and achieve the objectives that you originally set for the business.

Remember the Recycling mantra:

Review. Revise. Repeat.

YOU'VE LEARNED A LOT. KEEP USING IT.

Preparing a Business Plan will always force you to learn some things that you didn't even know you needed to know and it will deliver some results that you never expected.

For example, your Title Page will likely include the corporate name, logo and marketing slogan that you developed for your business plan. Now you can incorporate them into your business cards and stationery, brochures, websites, social media pages, and e-mail signature so that your business looks like it has already arrived.

You will now have an "Elevator Pitch" and be comfortable using it. "Hello, this is who I am, what I do and why it should matter to you." You'll be ready for every opportunity to promote your business with a 10-second pitch, a two minute version, a PowerPoint slide show, an e-mail intro and .pdf attachments.

You have probably enhanced your spreadsheet and financial analysis skills and have templates ready to assess and incorporate revisions into the business plan to account for any changes in the industry or marketing landscape. Your templates from this business plan can now be used for you next business expansion projects into new product lines or new markets.

And now that you've promoted yourself to a business plan "expert," you can start your next business venture or help someone else with theirs. Don't be shy to share your new knowledge. Like me, you will continue to learn in the process.

That concludes **The Complete Do-It-Yourself Guide to Business Plans - 2020 Edition.**

The rest is up to you. *Tuum est**.

* The motto of the University of British Columbia, my Engineering Alma Mater in Vancouver, B.C.

APPENDICES

THE PITCH

- RelaxStation
- Indie Author Direct
- WWW.Together

THE PLAN

- Happy Pets Center Inc.
- GO Freight Inc.

THE EXIT

- Boxco Manufacturing
- Service Co. Professional Services

THE PITCH

Following are three examples of a pitch for a new business idea. They are representative of what needs to be presented to potential business associates to test the idea and business concept and before preparing a formal business plan.

Each pitch provides a brief description of the market opportunity, the idea and the proposed strategy to build a viable business that responds to the defined opportunity.

RelaxStation – Your home office away from home

Pitch:
The current widespread use of crowded, noisy, uncomfortable coffee shops as workstations suggests there is an opportunity to provide a better facility and a more appealing environment. Better than the local coffee shop and better than the lonely home office or expensive shared office concept available to independent or self-employed workers. The RelaxStation concept will offer more relaxed but professional interaction with comprehensive access to more efficient office technology and workstations and separate areas for socializing and privacy.

The RelaxStation will operate like a real world version of Linkedin, designed for independent professionals with alternative levels of service from free to pay-as-you-play to monthly memberships with discounts on products and services.

Questions & Concerns:
One multi-purpose facility may be very expensive to build and the higher costs for visitors and members may not be acceptable even with the attraction of a better environment and additional services for work and relaxation.

Next Steps:
Test the concept with potential business partners in existing spaces – office buildings, retail/commercial centres, coffee shops and shared office concepts. Assess the potential to re-configure current independent locations. Test a first location to develop a standard business model and then consider franchising operations for RelaxStation.

Indie Author Direct – Matching new writers to readers

Pitch:
My experience as an author-preneur with Uncle Ralph's Publishing Empire has demonstrated the opportunity for providing better solutions to market and distribute the books of independent authors to interested readers. The proposal of Indie Author Direct is to organize a co-operative effort of indie authors supporting each other in marketing, distribution and sales for their books.

Traditional publishers and book resellers are too controlled and limiting for the ambitious independent author. They prefer to support primarily current best-selling writers or new writers who are already recognized celebrities, CEOs or politicians. They have very little incentive to invest in the selection and support of an unknown new author among the thousands that present books to the market every day.

Self-publishing is currently very easy and inexpensive and that means too many bad books are produced, simply because it's easy and inexpensive. Nobody verifies that the writer is worthy of any attention from the intended reader. Readers also have difficulty deciding who to trust with their time and money. They rely on reviews and recommendations from recognized authorities and other readers. So authors require reviews and recommendations to get sales.

The solution for more effective book marketing, distribution and sales is to create a channel dedicated to the selection and support of qualified indie authors that will more effectively introduce them to interested readers and booksellers.

Questions & Concerns:
Who will join and how many will be sufficient to test the concept. Why are current author services and solutions not working and can

they be fixed? How can Indie Author Direct successfully compete with traditional publishing and bookselling channels?

Next Steps:
Test the concept with indie authors and current author service businesses for book marketing and distribution. Select and develop the initial business partners to test the concept and develop a business plan.

WWW.Together – We.Work.Well.Together

Pitch:
Back to the future – with a portal/user interface that offers a web browser, search and e-mail services without the current overabundance of hazards and objections related to hacking, SPAM and junk mail, intrusive advertising and the privacy concerns that exist with current free online services.

Similar to the original Web portals that have all been replaced by the dominant players, like Google and Facebook, who aggressively capture private data to more effectively push advertising that is their primary source of revenue. Their comprehensive and pervasive "free" services come at a price that is not acceptable to everyone.

The services of WWW.Together would be user-supported like Wikipedia, but with a monthly subscription fee like Netflix or Amazon Prime to deliver a full range of services without the intrusive advertising or exploiting of private user data.

Questions & Concerns:
Most Internet users expect all these services for free and find the objections not sufficient to justify paying for use of the services. Development and operating costs would be huge and may require years of losses before achieving profitability.

Why are major technology players like Apple or Microsoft not offering this alternative already?

Next Steps:
Contact potential technology partners to test the concept and develop various business models with estimated budgets and timetables for development and operations. Prepare a joint business plan and pitch to venture capital sources for financing to support the initial years of negative cash flow before going global and becoming profitable.

THE PLAN

These two sample business plans are presented to give you clear examples of the recommended content and presentation style for your own business plan. The Happy Pets Center is a typical retail business and GO Freight is a typical professional services business.

Your business may be similar to neither of those examples, but the specific facts and figures are less important than learning from the overall presentation of strategy and plans. Note, in particular, the content and tone that confirms the confidence and enthusiasm of the entrepreneurs as well as their relevant knowledge and experience, competence, conviction and commitment. Those are the key elements that will respond to the questions and concerns of potential lenders and investors.

Both sample business plans follow the same recommended outline and include some standard language that is expected by critical readers. It may seem boring and irrelevant to you, but it is important to anyone interested in your business. You should anticipate their questions and also demonstrate your ability to communicate effectively with people who are unfamiliar with your industry or technology. Don't be too creative or radical for the conservative bankers and investors whom you are trying to persuade to have confidence in your ability to deliver the results that you're planning.

Similarly, the financial projections and appendices may not all be pertinent or relevant for your own business plans, but they will give you some guidelines for the format and content that is expected. Supporting detail may be kept aside for follow-up questions or the next level of review and summary data is usually sufficient for the initial presentation of your business plan.

Remember, a business plan document of fifteen to twenty pages, including appendices, should adequately describe the plans for a relatively simple business seeking less than one million dollars in financing. If you are more ambitious and seeking more significant funding, the short version business plan is still a very useful starting point for introduction to new business partners and sources of financing.

It was an iterative process to prepare the business plan and it will be a similar process to present it. Start with a one page overview of the concept and business model, expand on it with an Executive Summary and Pitch, then present a short version Business Plan and organize all the supporting documentation for subsequent more comprehensive review of the details.

These sample business plans will help you understand what your final documents should look like at the end of the process in order for you to get the results you hope to achieve.

Business Plan - Happy Pets Center Inc.

(<u>Note</u>: Actual client names and information have been changed to protect their confidentiality.)

Purpose:

This Business Plan documents the strategies and plans for expansion of Happy Pets Center Inc. in order to provide potential investors and other sources of financing with the information required to evaluate the business opportunity and to confirm the financial requirements to proceed with the plan.

Prepared By: Diane Howe, President, **Happy Pets Center Inc.**

Assisted By: Del Chatterson, Consultant, LearningEntrepreneurship.com

<u>*Disclaimer:*</u> *LearningEntrepreneurship.com and its Consultants make no warranties or representations as to the validity of facts, forecasts and assumptions, or the viability of the plan.*

<u>*Notice:*</u> *This business plan contains information that is confidential to the company and its owners. It is not to be shared or copied without their prior consent. The reader further acknowledges that he/she has no conflicting personal or business interests.*

Copy # __ Accepted and receipt acknowledged by:

Signed _____ Date: _____

To the reader

Thank you for your interest in our Business Plan which presents the strategies and plans for the expansion of our business. Please note that it is a confidential document between us and subject to the terms of the Non-Disclosure Agreement attached as Appendix A.

We are asking you to review this Business Plan for the purpose of your considering participation in financing the expansion of Happy Pets. The business has been financed to date by the current shareholders and internal cash flow. Full realization of the business opportunities attainable through expansion will require additional financing as described in this Business Plan.

Please contact us directly if you have further questions or wish to arrange a follow-up meeting after reviewing the Business Plan. We appreciate your interest in our plans.

Yours truly,

Diane Howe, President.

Happy Pets Center Inc.

BUSINESS PLAN - TABLE OF CONTENTS

APPENDICES

(Not included in this sample, except for financial projections.)

1. Executive summary

Happy Pets Center Inc. currently operates a storefront business on ABC Street in West Town and is planning to expand its facilities and services to a larger pet center. The new pet center will be an easily accessible destination located in the South Park commercial area with about 9000 sq. ft. of space including a retail storefront for sale of pet nutrition, supplies and accessories, a veterinary clinic for diagnosis and treatment of pets and additional facilities for pet grooming.

The Happy Pets approach has been developed and proven over the last 3-1/2 years and demand for our services continues to grow. The current facility is stretched beyond its capacity and competing pet stores are expanding their services to respond to the demonstrated market opportunities. It is timely for Happy Pets to build on its established credibility and maintain its leadership position.

The new facility will require additional financing of approximately $235,000 over the next four to six months for the necessary capital equipment, leasehold improvements and start-up expenses. This new Happy Pets Pet Center is expected to achieve satisfactory profitability within two years at a projected revenue of $2 million per year.

The following Business Plan provides more details on the business concept, strategy, operating plans and financial projections.

2. Concept and business opportunity

Happy Pets Center Inc. is a business dedicated to promoting and supporting the care of domestic pets. Our approach to pet care is growing in importance as consumers and pet owners become more aware of the requirements for adequate pet care and of the difference that good care can make to owning healthier and happier family pets.

Currently, Happy Pets operates a small retail outlet on ABC Street in West Town offering pet nutrition and accessory products, grooming services and limited veterinary care. This storefront operation opened six years ago and has demonstrated the growing demand for healthy and ethical pet nutrition products and services.

This Business Plan addresses the opportunity for an expanded pet center in a new facility. The new center will be in a more accessible location allowing it to become the regional destination for quality pet care. It will attract and be able to serve a much larger clientele. It will continue to focus on high quality natural pet nutrition products and services. It will also offer a wide range of complementary products and services including health remedies, food diets, supplements, pet accessories and supplies, grooming services, and limited veterinary care.

Market demand for Happy Pets type of pet care is growing with the trends to increasing consumer demand for natural food and health care products and with the increasing public awareness of issues related to the proper care and treatment of their animals. These issues receive continuous attention in the media – product safety, animal testing, use of chemicals and additives in food products, inadequate health and safety standards. Just as consumers become more demanding for their own health and well-being they also recognize the importance of these issues in the care and nutrition of their pets. Although major brand-name suppliers continue to supply pet shops with their generic pet foods, they have recognized the growing consumer demand and are responding effectively with more natural and ethical products.

Happy Pets is very focused on catering to the needs for natural pet nutrition and healthy pet care by providing better information, products and services than any other pet care store in Canada. The principals in Happy Pets have well recognized reputations for their expertise and integrity in pet care and this distinguishes them from any competitor. Pet care products are available from a wide variety of sources – high volume national retailers to the local pet shop. But no one else can offer the level of expertise and dedication to healthy pet care that are available from the management and staff of Happy Pets.

This combination of growing demand and lack of credible suppliers presents a continuing business opportunity that must be addressed by Happy Pets before a direct competitor can establish itself in the target market. Customer demand for products and services at the existing Happy Pets outlet already exceeds the capacity of the store. More space, expanded inventory, additional facilities and services combined with easier access with free parking will allow the business to support demand from the metropolitan area and beyond. An effective marketing campaign will quickly build traffic to the new location and deliver sales revenues in line with our projections.

The Business Plan for expansion addresses this business opportunity and demonstrates the profit potential for investors. Our objective is to grow from current sales of approximately $300,000 per year at the current store to achieve additional sales at an expanded pet center exceeding $2,000,000 per year within three years. We will achieve these goals by maintaining a dedication to healthy pet care and providing a complete range of products and services that meet growing consumer demand.

3. Mission statement

Happy Pets is committed to becoming the Canadian leader in healthy pet care. The company's mission is to:

- ❑ Educate – creating awareness of healthy choices in pet nutrition and care.
- ❑ Prevent – providing products and services to ensure the long term well-being of pets.
- ❑ Heal – offering a basic range of veterinary services to cure pet ailments.

Adherence to these principles will guide the business stategies and operating practices of Happy Pets in its expansion plans.

4. Market analysis

Market Opportunity

American pet food sales were $13.64 billion last year. Manufacturers' sales growth was 3.6%. Organic pet food sales were estimated at $32 million in 2004 and growing. (Ref.: Pet Age, February 20..)

The IAMS Company, owned by Procter & Gamble has global sales of $1.3 billion in 70 countries and is the No. 1 brand name in the United States. The company has grown from its start in 1950 by focusing on higher quality pet nutrition. Other pet food manufacturers are also catering to higher quality demands and developing products for more specific pet requirements.

In spite of generally poor general retail sales at the end of last year, the pet industry had more positive results. Two large U.S. retailers, PETCO and PetsMART had third quarter sales increases of 7.0% and 6.7%. Pet owners continue to spend generously on their animals with annual expanditures of $416 per year by cat owners and $475 per year by dog owners according to a recent APPMA National Pet Owners Survey in the U.S.

The survey indicates that 40% of that spending goes on pet food. 35% of pet owners shop in supermarkets and spend an average of $8.99 to $14.99 for a 20-lb. bag of dog food. Premium brands are selling at $35.00 per 40-lb. bag. Pet owners also spend an average of $50 (Minimum of $45 for small dogs, up to $90 for large dogs) per grooming, $20-$30 per day for daycare, and costs for veterinary services run from $100 per visit for fees and remedies up to to several hundreds, even thousands of dollars, for tests, medication, surgery and follow-up care. (Ref.: *Pet Business*, February 20..)

Pet retailers have recognized the business expansion opportunities of catering to pet owners needs and are introducing additional services such as grooming, daycare, pet walking, training classes, and pet tharapy. Their efforts also include building brand loyalty and demonstrating social responsibility by participating in adoption clinics, animal welfare events and contributing to animal rescue organisations.

The concept of providing healthier natural pet care initiated by Happy Pets is starting to be imitated by some new local competitors: Big Doggy (2 stores), Masters Pet (3 stores), Bark and Meow (a new franchise), and also some existing stores: Three Bears, Klub K-9 and Martin Pets. Their intiatives help to confirm the interest in healthier pet care services and reinforce the strategy of protecting our leadership position by taking the concept to the next level with a larger integrated pet center.

Previous analysis of the Canadian pet care market in our original Business Plan of 20.. indicated Canadian pet care spending averaging approximately $400 per year on 4.5 million cats and 3.5 million dogs in Canada. (*Statistics Canada – 20..*) Based on a regional population of at least 3.5 million in the area served by the new pet center, and assuming the same spending per year and the same ratio of pets to total population (8/30 million), the total pet care market in the region is estimated at $373 million per year. If 5% of that market is seeking natural, premium grade products and healthier pet care, then the total market potential for Happy Pets is $18.65 million.

We are confident that the new Happy Pets Center can achieve satisfactory profitability and return on investment at $2,000,000 in sales which would represent an estimated 10.7% market share within two years.

Target Markets
Pet owners who are concerned about animal health and welfare and have a preference for natural products and a healthy approach to care, prevention and treatment are the most relevant prospective customers for Happy Pets. These pet owners currently represent about 5% of total Canadian spending on pet nutrition and health care.

Customer needs
Customer characteristics that favour Happy Pets are the need for information, integrity, and consistency in the offering of healthy natural products and pet care services. These are the competitive advantages of Happy Pets.

Buying process
Customers have found Happy Pets through various means – walk by traffic, press coverage, follow-up to magazine articles and referrals from veterinarians, health practitioners and health food stores.

As they become aware of the issues, pet care alternatives and the availability of the Happy Pets Center pet owners become customers, then advocates and strong referral sources by word-of-mouth marketing.

The choice of a new location with easy highway access and adequate free parking will make the pet centre a regional destination for all healthy pet care needs. (Public transit is less important.)

5. Competition

The U.S. market is dominated by two national chains, PETSCO and PetSmart with a total of 1400 outlets and combined sales exceeding $5 billion. Both chains are expanding rapidly and expected to win customers and sales volume from both independent retailers and the supermarkets. Industry experts expect that the smaller, regional chains will be most vulnerable to the powerful economies of scale while the owner-operated specialty retailer will be able to retain customers with a closer personal touch and focused product lines.

The third largest pet retailer is Pet Value of Markham Ontario with 350 outlets in Ontario and Manitoba and the U.S. Mid-Atlantic region. About 120 units are franchisees and most are located in 1200 to 2500 sq. ft. near a neighbourhood shopping mall. None of the larger franchises are yet in Quebec, deterred by the usual language and cultural issues, but they are likely to be present soon given the size of the Quebec market and the lack of high profile branded competitors.

Petcetera is another growing and successful pet retailer in Canada opening in Vancouver in 1997 and now operating 37 stores in five provinces. They are also dedicated to animal welfare and provide services to support animal adoption of 500 – 800 dogs and cats per month. In the interest of animal welfare they do not sell live dogs, cats or exotic pets.

Most independent pet retailers try to offer a full range of products. None have the integrity and dedication to natural/healthy/ethical products that will continue to distinguish Happy Pets from its competitors. Furthermore, Happy Pets is known and recognized by its retail peers, local veterinarians and the public for having the professional expertise and experience that sets it apart as Canada's leader in complete healthy pet care.

The current most significant competitors to Happy Pets are:

❏ ABC, established for many years, it would appear to be comparable to Happy Pets in the type of products, size and style of operation, and type of clientele. Not conveniently or centrally located it is probably limited to the local residential area of pet owners.

❏ Bark & Meow, an Ontario franchise, just recently opened, its success is not yet established.

- Three Bears, owned by two women partners, who are its second owners, they have a reputation for poor customer service and lack of expertise. They are not expected to survive.

- CDK In operation for at least eight years by its original owners, their sales probably rival those of Happy Pets. Their product lines and setup are similar to those of Three Bears, although their store is approximately three times the size.

As Happy Pets has succeeded in the local market, its competitors have responded with the addition of "natural" products to their inventory. But these competitors will require time or large promotional expenditures to establish their credibility and build customer awareness.

Competition at various levels will continue to exist from the full range of national retailers, local pet shops, private groomers and pet therapists, and traditional veterinarians. However, the unique positioning and competitive strengths of Happy Pets will allow us to retain significant market share, grow and build a successful, profitable business.

6. Strategic plan
Business History
Founded by Diane Howe and partners, the current storefront was opened September 10, 2005. Since then, it has established a loyal and enthusiastic clientele and built solid relations with key suppliers. (See testimonials in Appendix J)

Ownership and Management
Happy Pets Center, Inc. is a legal entity federally incorporated and registered in the province of Quebec, Canada. It is currently owned 100% by Diane Howe. A plan is in place to have the other key members of the management team, acquire up to 10% each in the new business, prior to the issuing of additional shares to any major new investor(s). A binding contract between all three parties will be drawn up to ensure a lasting and exclusive business relationship.

Intellectual Property Protection
No current products or processes have been developed that require protection by patent or copyright. The company name is in the process of being trademarked for the potential use of "Happy Pets" on future branded products.

Regulatory Issues / Certifications
In order to operate a veterinary clinic, that part of the business must be under the ownership and control of a registered veterinarian. Pet groomers do not require any specific certification or licencing. Other standard retail business licencing requirements will be met in the new location.

Current strategic position

Happy Pets is seen by customers, competitors and suppliers as a strong advocate and knowledgeable source for natural pet care products and healthy treatment of pets. That reputation adds credibility and brand value to the new pet center.

Strategic Objectives

Following are the key strategic objectives for the expansion plan:

1. Establish sustainable and profitable businesses processes at the current store to achieve annual sales of $500,000, adequate return to the owner, and net income of $30,000 per year by September 30, Year 1.

2. Complete negotiations for new equity and debt financing to support the expansion plan by June 30, Year 1.

3. Complete the expansion project to open the new Pet Center premises by October 31, Year 1.

4. Achieve sustainable annual sales at the new Pet Center of $1,500,000 per year by September 30, Year 2.

5. Achieve annual sales at the new Pet Center of $2,500,000 per year by September 30, Year 5 with net profit after tax of $150,000 per year.

6. Open two new storefront operations (franchised or owned); one by March and another by September, Year 3.

7. Expand distribution rights for selected nutrition products to achieve annual distribution sales exceeding $100,000 per year by September 30, Year 3.

8. Begin research and development for production of Happy Pets lines of pet food and supplements by January Year 4.

Strategic Action Plan

1. Make initial presentations of the Business Plan to bank lenders and potential new investors by March 31, Year 1.

2. Identify the preferred sources of financing and confirm the general arrangements by May 31, Year 1.

3. Finalize negotiations for financing and initiate the plans for leasing new premises by June 30, Year 1.

4. Complete the leasehold improvements and installation of capital equipment to open the new Pet Center by October 31, Year 1.

5. Develop and launch a marketing plan that coincides with the opening of the new Pet Center and drives initial traffic to the new location.

6. Manage the Pet Center to deliver the forecast revenues and profits in the strategic plan.

7. Management team

A primary competitive strength of Happy Pets arises from the combined knowledge, skills and experience of its management team.

The key members who are dedicated to achieving the company's objectives are:

Diane Howe, President

She is a well-known and respected authority on pet products, healthy pet care and the ethical treatment of animals. He is a regular contributor to a variety of publications on these subjects. He also has experience in sales and marketing of natural pet nutrition products prior to opening Happy Pets and has been active in promoting and managing the current retail store to ensure its profitable growth since opening in 2001.

Mr. Smooth Fur

He is a well-trained and experienced pet groomer as well as an active supporter of pet welfare. He has been active in providing pet grooming services at Happy Pets since March, 2003. He has also assisted in the physical setup of the current location.

Dr. Healthy Pets

She is a licenced doctor of veterinary science and a knowledgeable supporter of natural and ethical nutrition and pet care products. She has been active in support and guidance to management and staff since the initial opening of Happy Pets. She has also assisted in the planning and design of the new pet center.

Background information and the credentials of each of these individuals are provided in more detail in Appendix D along with an initial organizational structure. Additional experienced resources are also known to the management team and will be engaged in appropriate positions as they are required.

The organizational plan and the associated staffing costs are presented with the financial schedules of Appendix C.

8. Product and service offering

The new pet center will allow expansion of the products and services already available from the current storefront on ABC Street.

THE COMPLETE DO-IT-YOURSELF GUIDE TO BUSINESS PLANS

Pet Nutrition:
- ❏ Certified, all natural, high quality pet food
- ❏ Dietary supplements
- ❏ Veterinary remedies

Pet supplies and accessories:
- ❏ Leashes, beds, bowls
- ❏ Pet clothing
- ❏ Souvenirs, cards, calendars
- ❏ Books and magazines

Pet care products:
- ❏ All natural shampoos
- ❏ Hygeine products
- ❏ Natural, non-toxic cleaning products.

Pet care services:
- ❏ grooming
- ❏ behavioral therapy
- ❏ Therapeutic pet massage

Health and veterinary services:
- ❏ Diagnosis and treatment of animal illness and disease
- ❏ accupuncture and accupressure
- ❏ Chiropractic service
- ❏ Physiotherapy

Future products and services

Happy Pets is in constant growth and development for both new products and services. These include foods, accessories, and services. Although we currently cover all possible healthy pet care services, there is the potential to add pet day care, hotel-style boarding and dog walking services.

9. Marketing and sales plan

The marketing strategy for Happy Pets Center will target the specific market niche of pet owners interested in natural products for nutrition and healthy treatments for pet care.

The positioning strategy will emphasis the integrity and qualifications of Happy Pets in the field of healthy pet care. It will emphasize the knowledge and experience advantages of Happy Pets over other sources of pet nutrition and healthy pet care. The management team will continue to be active in advocacy and public relations for natural pet nutrition, healthy treatment and the ethical treatment of animals. The strong media interest in these subjects has provided good exposure for Happy Pets in the past. (See Appendix K.)

To maintain our competitive advantage, sales and service staff will be screened to ensure their attitudes and interests are in line with the mission of Happy Pets. Training will provide them with the necessary knowledge to help inform customers and assist in their pet care decisions.

A limited number of products will be sold and they will continue to be carefully selected from suppliers that meet our criteria for high quality, natural products and ethical business practices.

Advertising and promotion activities for the new pet center will include health and pet oriented publications and events more than the general media. The company and its management team will be active in sponsorship and participation for SPCA activities, pet adoption, and by organizing fund raising events for pet shelters in various boroughs.

A strong referral network will be built with local veterinary clinics and health food stores to direct interested customers to Happy Pets. Appropriate marketing materials will be made available to these locations. Some incentive programs may need to be developed to encourage these sources of referrals.

Pet industry trade shows and other industry events will be attended to promote Happy Pets both locally and internationally and to develop important relationships with other participants in healthy pet care.

10. Operations plan

Location and Facilities

Happy Pets is currently located on ABC Street in West Town. Since it is the only pet supply store in the region dedicated to natural pet nutrition and healthy pet care with such strong qualifications, expertise and credibility, it draws customers from many miles away. Inquiries for access to our unique products and servicse have been received from across Canada, the U.S. and the U.K.

A review of the current active customer list indicates a particularly large distribution of customers from the South Park area. This factor has influenced the interest in selecting a new location in South Park.

The new facility is planned for approximately 8000 - 9000 square feet of space with about 4000 sq. ft. dedicated to the retail store, 1300 for the veterinary clinic, 1200 sq. ft. for for grooming. A small office will be required at about 150 sq. ft., a small kitchenette with two tables at about 250-300 sq. ft. Obedience/dog training classes or hosting other courses/activities, will need an area designated for such purposes; aproximately 600-800 square feet. Additional space for washrooms and common areas indicate a minimum requirement of about 8000 sq. ft. An initial general layout of the facilities is provided in Appendix H.

Operating Processes

The retail portion of the new pet center will be open for normal operating hours of Monday to Wednesday 9:00am – 6:00pm; Thursday and Friday 9:00am – 9:00pm; Saturday and Sunday 10:00am – 5:00pm. The clinic will be open Monday to Friday from 9:00am to 7:00pm.

Staffing will include well-trained and motivated retail sales clerks compensated with appropriate base salaries and a shared commission plan for additional incentive.

Mr. Smooth Fur will manage the groomers as independent contractors paid on a per cent of fees earned. He will also be charged a monthly allocation for the use of premises.

Dr. Healthy Pets will be available for consultation and scheduling of appointments during regular store hours.

Current suppliers will be retained and the new facility will make it easier to accommodate and expand the distribution business for resale of selected product lines to other pet retailers. This could become more significant if addressed as a separate business opportunity but will require additional investment to do so.

For many current customers the new facility will be much more convenient to access and pick up products. Sales volume per customer should increase accordingly. The existing store may see some sales decline but the impact can be offset by reducing the hours of service. It is also expected that our marketing programs will have a spillover effect and drive new traffic to the existing store. It will remain open as a model site and training location for other storefront operations.

11. Risk analysis

The investment risks are understood and will be managed to the minimum possible. These risks arise from both market or economic conditions that are not controllable by Happy Pets and from business conditions that are internal to Happy Pets.

Market risks:
1. Decline of overall market.
   Trends do not suggest any likely decline of the overall market for pet supplies. Risk to Happy Pets is limited by its relatively small but growing market share and its ability to compensate for any general market decline by increasing its market share.

2. New competitors.
   Potential exists for new competitors, but Happy Pets has the opportunity to create a market leadership position in its chosen niche of healthy pet care.

3. New market requirements.
   It is unlikely that the trends toward natural products and healthy health care will suddenly shift to new approaches. This is not a short-term fashion or fad concept.

Business risks:
1. Availability of key personnel
   Happy Pets will offer opportunities for profit participation as an incentive to retain key management staff and also have signed employment contracts that provide protection from abrupt termination by either party. Operating employees will not be unionized so mass withdrawal of services is unlikely.

2. Loss of suppliers
   Protection of supply will be achieved by negotiated contract terms and by maintaining alternative sources.

3. Systems and facilities risks
   Happy Pets will take reasonable precautions to protect systems and facilities and also maintain commercial insurance against business interruption.

3. Regulatory
   Happy Pets will maintain and upgrade all regulatory approvals as necessary.

The financial projections show that Happy Pets's business model has strong revenue potential that is attractive in spite of normal business risks.

12. Financial plan

A detailed financial plan is attached as Appendix A.
The Financial Plan includes the following:

A. Summary of financial results to date for the current store.

B. Financial projections for the current store

C. Financial Forecasts for the expanded Healthy Pet Center:
   - Opening Balance Sheet and Financial Requirements
   - Capital Expenditures and Leasehold Improvements
   - Sales Revenue and Gross Profit Projections
   - Organisation Plan
   - Expense Forecast
   - Net Income and ROI Projections
   - Cash Flow Forecast
   - Investment Forecast
   - Projected Balance Sheets

This Business Plan has been prepared to describe the business opportunity, the strategy, the operating plan, and the expected financial results.
Thank you for your interest in reviewing it.

- - - - - - - -

Financial Projections – Happy Pets Center Inc.

The financial projections for Happy Pets Center Inc. are shown in the following pages. They include:

- ❏ Initial Balance Sheet showing the start-up costs and planned sources of financing
- ❏ Sales, Revenue and Gross Margin forecasts
- ❏ Variable and fixed expenses, Profit and Loss Projections and an estimate of equity value
- ❏ Cash Flow Projections
- ❏ Balance Sheet Projections
- ❏ Notes on the assumptions used and the basis for all the estimated values

These example projections will give you some ideas on how to present your own financials. You can then develop spreadsheets to evaluate various scenarios and assumptions, until you are satisfied with the planned results.

Be sure to check your final draft so that the business plan text is consistent with the financial results that you show in your Appendices.

Table 1

Expansion Start-up Requirements	Opening Balance Sheet	Required for Start-up*	Total
ASSETS			
Cash	5,000	0	5,000
Inventory	0	65,000	65,000
Accounts Receivable	0		0
Advances Receivable	0		0
Capital Equipment (net)	0		0
Leasehold improvements*	0	69,850	69,850
Incorporation	1,500	0	1,500
Capital Equipment Sub-total	**1,500**	**69,850**	**71,350**
PRE-PAID EXPENSES			
Financing costs	1,500	985	2,485
Professional fees	7,500	10,000	17,500
Start-up expense & deposits	5,000	7,000	12,000
Expense Sub-total:	14,000	17,985	31,985
Total Funding Requirements	**20,500**	**152,835**	**173,335**
SOURCES OF FINANCING			
Current liabilities	0		0
Current bank loans	10,500	0	10,500
Shareholder loans	0	0	0
New lending		120,000	120,000
Retained Earnings	0		0
Shareholder Capital	10,000	0	10,000
New Equity Investment		32,835	32,835
Total Equity	10,000	32,835	42,835
Total Financing	**20,500**	**152,835**	**173,335**

* Details of expansion start-up costs attached.

Table 2

CAPITAL EXPENDITURES	Start-up Costs	Year 2	Year 3
Retail Store area: (4000 sq. ft.)			
Shelving	$ 7,250.00		
Interior décor	$ 1,200.00		
Cash register with scanner	$ 2,250.00		
Inventory Control software	$ 5,000.00		$ 500.00
Office computers & equip.	$ 2,500.00	$ 1,500.00	
SUB-TOTAL	**$ 18,200.00**	**$ 1,500.00**	**$ 500.00**
Reception area (480 sq.ft.)	$ 5,000.00		
Washrooms (2) (100 sq.ft.)	$ 2,000.00		
Veterinary office & equip. (150 sq.ft.)	$ 7,000.00		
SUB-TOTAL	**$ 14,000.00**	**-**	**-**
Hydraulic tables (2)	$ 4,000.00		
Kennels (2)	$ 4,000.00		
Other equipment, furnishings	$ 950.00	$ 1,500.00	$ 1,500.00
SUB-TOTAL:	**$ 8,950.00**	**$ 1,500.00**	**$ 1,500.00**
Class Room Furniture & Equipment (seating 20)	$ 3,700.00		$ 1,500.00
Signage	$ 5,000.00		
Furnishing & fixtures	$ 12,500.00	$ 1,500.00	$ 1,500.00
Interior decoration	$ 7,500.00		
SUB-TOTAL	**$ 25,000.00**	**$ 1,500.00**	**$ 1,500.00**
TOTAL CAPITAL EXPENDITURES	**$ 69,850.00**	**$ 4,500.00**	**$ 5,000.00**

Table 3

SALES REVENUE FORECASTS PET CENTRE	Monthly sales	Start-up 3-mos	Year 1	Year 2	Year 3
Sales - nutrition	Monthly	2	Growth @	30%	15%
Revenue	$ 50,000	100.0	550.0	715.0	822.3
Sales - pet accessories	Monthly	2			
Revenue @ 30% of food	$ 15,000	30.0	165.0	214.5	246.7
Grooming services	hours	300			
Fees @ $50/hour	$ 50	15.0	87.0	113.1	130.1
Veterinary Services	hours	320			
Fees @ $115/hr	$ 115	36.8	202.4	263.1	302.6
Veterinary Care Products	Monthly				
Revenue @ 50% of fees	50%	18.4	101.2	131.6	151.3
Nutritional Supplements	Monthly	2			
Revenue	$ 17,500	35.0	192.5	250.3	287.8
Other: therapy, classes, etc.		2			
Revenue @ $250/class	$ 250	0.5	2.8	3.6	4.1
TOTAL REVENUE		**235.7**	**1300.9**	**1691.1**	**1944.8**
PRODUCT COSTS	% of sales				
Nutrition products	65%	65.0	357.5	464.8	534.5
Accessories	55%	16.5	90.8	118.0	135.7
Groomers cost	50%	7.5	43.5	56.6	65.0
Hydro-therapist costs	50%	0.0	0.0	0.0	0.0
Veterinarian	75%	27.6	151.8	197.3	226.9
Vet. Product costs	60%	11.0	60.7	78.9	90.8
Nutritional Supplements	65%	22.8	125.1	162.7	187.1
Transport & stocking	0.5%	0.9	5.0	6.6	7.5
Sales commissions	0.0%	0.0	0.0	0.0	0.0
Total Cost of Sales		**151.3**	**834.4**	**1084.8**	**1247.5**
GROSS MARGIN $		**84.4**	**466.4**	**606.3**	**697.3**
Gross Margin %		**35.8%**	**35.9%**	**35.9%**	**35.9%**

Table 4

ORGANIZATION PLAN		Year 1	Year 2	Year 3
NO. OF PLANNED STAFF				
General Manager		1	1	1
Store Manager		1	1	1
Retail Sales staff*		4	4	6
Finance & Admin.		1	1	1
Clinic receptionist		1	1	1
Veterinary technician		1	1.5	1.5
TOTAL STAFF		**9**	**9.5**	**11.5**
EXPENSE/EMPLOYEE	Annual Salary	Monthly Expense ($ 1000s)		
General Manager	$ 40,000	3.8	3.8	3.8
Store Manager	$ 35,000	3.4	3.4	3.4
Retail Sales staff*	$ 20,800	2.0	2.0	2.0
Finance & Admin.	$ 35,000	3.4	3.4	3.4
Clinic receptionist	$ 24,000	2.3	2.3	2.3
Veterinary technician	$ 30,000	2.9	2.9	2.9
		Annual Expense ($ 1000s)		
General Manager		46.0	46.0	46.0
Store Manager		40.3	40.3	40.3
Retail Sales staff*		95.7	95.7	143.5
Finance & Admin.		40.3	40.3	40.3
Clinic receptionist		27.6	27.6	27.6
Veterinary technician		34.5	51.8	51.8
TOTAL ANNUAL COSTS		**284.3**	**301.5**	**349.4**

*Note: Retail sales staff @ average $10.00/hour and all staff plus 15% for benefits.

Table 5

EXPENSE FORECAST	Start-up 3-mos	Year 1	Year 2	Year 3
OPERATING EXPENSE				
*Total Staff	9	9	9.5	11.5
*Total Staff Costs	71.1	284.3	301.5	349.4
Admin. & Office Expense @% Staff 5.0%	3.6	14.2	15.1	17.5
Pre-paid Start-up Expenses	31.99	32.0		
Rent paid	24.75	99.0	102.0	105.0
Rent Inc. from Vet. Clinic & Grooming		0.0	0.0	0.0
Business Insurance & Taxes	3.0	12.0	12.0	15.0
Telecom/Internet, Utilities	2.3	9.0	9.0	12.0
Professional Fees	3.0	9.5	9.5	12.5
Total O/H & Admin.	**68.5**	**175.7**	**147.5**	**162.0**
Sales & Marketing				
Marketing materials	2.5	4.0	7.5	7.5
Advertising & Promotion	7.5	21.0	25.0	30.0
Web Site Maintenance		6.5	2.5	2.5
Total Sales & Mktg. Exp.	10.0	31.5	35.0	40.0
TOTAL OPERATING EXPENSE	**149.6**	**491.5**	**484.1**	**551.4**

* See Organization Plan for details.

Table 6

SUMMARY - NET INCOME ($ 1000s)	Start-up 3-mos	Year 1	Year 2	Year 3
		$	$	$
TOTAL REVENUE	235.7	1300.9	1691.1	1944.8
Total Cost of Sales	151.3	834.4	1084.7	1247.4
GROSS MARGIN $	84.4	466.4	606.3	697.3
Gross Margin %	35.8%	35.9%	35.9%	35.9%
OPERATING EXPENSE				
*Total Staff Costs:	71.1	284.3	301.5	349.4
Total O/H & Admin.	68.5	175.7	147.5	162.0
Sales & Mktg Expense	10	31.5	35.0	40.0
Bank charges & Interest @ 6.0%	2.6	9.8	-1.2	-4.2
Depreciation	0.0	14.3	15.2	16.2
Total Expense	152.2	515.5	498.1	563.4
NET INCOME Before Tax	-67.8	-49.1	108.3	133.9
Net Income %:	-29%	-3.8%	6.4%	6.9%
Less income taxes @ 18.0%		-8.8	19.5	24.1
Net Income after tax:		- 40.28	88.77	109.81
Return on Total Assets		- 0.20	0.26	0.21
Return on Equity:		- 0.94	2.07	2.56
Net Present Value of 5-years discounted @20%		- 33.57	61.65	63.55
BUSINESS VALUE	**$ 91,627**			

* See attached Schedules for details
** Net Income before income tax.

107

Table 7

CASH FLOW FORECAST	Opening Balances	Year 1	Year 2	Year 3
MONTHLY RECEIPTS				
Initial cash balance	5.0	0.0		
Additional sources		0.0		
Cash received from sales		1300.9	1691.1	1944.8
TOTAL CASH INFLOW		**1300.9**	**1691.1**	**1944.8**
CASH PAYMENTS				
Total Cost of Sales		834.4	1084.8	1247.5
Monthly Operating Exp.		491.5	484.1	551.4
Capital & Start-up Costs		173.3	4.5	5.0
Income Taxes		-8.8	19.5	24.1
Dividends paid		0.0	0.0	0.0
TOTAL CASH OUTFLOW		**1490.4**	**1592.8**	**1828.0**
CASH SURPLUS/SHORT		**-189.6**	**98.3**	**116.8**
ADDITIONAL CASH IN				
Shareholders' Equity	10.0	10.0	0.0	0.0
Additional Equity	32.8	32.8	0.0	0.0
CUM. EQUITY:	**42.8**	**42.8**	**42.8**	**42.8**
Bank Loans	10.5	10.5	0.0	0.0
Shareholder loans	0.0	0.0	0.0	0.0
Additional financing	120.0	0.0	-150.0	-50.0
CUM. DEBT:	**130.5**	**130.5**	**-19.5**	**-69.5**
NET CASH FLOW(+/-)		**-136.2**	**98.3**	**116.8**
CUM. CASH BALANCE(+/-):	**5.0**	**-11.2**	**87.0**	**203.9**

Table 8

PROJECTED BALANCE SHEET ($ 1000s)	Opening Balance Sheet	Year 1	Year 2	Year 3
ASSETS				
Cash	5.0	-11.2	87.0	203.9
Inventory	65.0	216.8	281.9	324.1
Accounts Receivable	0.0	0.0	0.0	0.0
Advances Receivable	0.0	0.0	0.0	0.0
Capital Equipment	71.4	71.4	75.9	80.9
Less Depreciation @ avg. 20%	0.0	14.3	15.2	16.2
Net Capital Assets:	71.4	57.1	60.7	64.7
TOTAL ASSETS	**141.4**	**262.7**	**429.6**	**592.7**
Liabilities				
Short-term liabilities	-32.0	129.6	357.8	461.0
Bank loans	130.5	130.5	-19.5	-69.5
Shareholders Loans	0.0			
Shareholders' Equity	42.8	42.8	42.8	42.8
Cum. Retained Earnings	0.0	-40.3	48.5	158.3
TOTAL LIABILITIES	**141.4**	**262.7**	**429.6**	**592.7**

Notes to the Financial Projections:

1. Start-up costs are detailed in the attached schedule of capital expenditures and leasehold improvements. Assumed future expenditures are estimates of the expansion needs for upgrades and replacements.

2. Revenue projections are based on the sales factors applied to each revenue category for the periods indicated. Pet nutrition is the primary revenue generator at approximately 57% of total annual sales. The relationship between revenue categories shown in the monthly sales factors is based on current experience.

3. Sales per square foot for pet food and accessories is $268 per square foot in the new retail pet center versus $237per sq. ft. in the current store.

4. Grooming services are estimated at $50 per hour with two groomers working 20 hours per week to generate $8000 per month in Year 1. Each groomer will average four groomings per day.

5. Therapy services are estimated at an average $70/hour ($40 minimum ½ hour and $60/hour). The area is forecast to be used 4 hours per day, 4 days per week in the first year for 64 hours per month and $4480 in revenue.

6. Veterinary services are estimated to generate average fees of $115 per hour and average billings of six hours per day per vet. We have assumed one veterinarian available at 120 hours per month, plus another junior vet or technician available 40 hours per month generating the same average fee rate. Veterinary care products have historically generated additional revenue at 50% of the veterinary fees.

7. Distribution revenue is currently a small part of the business and is forecast to grow to only $200,000 per year within five years. This may be addressed as a separate business opportunity in the future.

8. The start-up phase of three months in the new pet center is estimated to generate approximately two months of normal revenue.

9. Year 2 nutrition revenue is estimated to grow at 30% over Year 1 with subsequent years growing at 15%. Other categories are forecast to grow proportionally. Revenue estimates do not include any provision for inflation or escalation of fee rates and do not include sales taxes collected or paid.

10. Gross margin calculations are based on historical costs for products, services and selling expenses from prior years. Veterinarians and groomers are paid at 85% and 50% of their fees, respectively. The veterinary clinic will also pay rent for the premises as indicated in the expense deduction of Schedule 3.

11. Staffing costs are based on the full-time employee equivalent hours and the salary rates as indicated. Benefits are estimated at 15% over base salaries. The management team is included in these costs at estimated market values for the services provided by each. Retail sales staff are increased in the third year and staff for distribution are added when sales reach $100,000 per year.

12. Overhead and administrative expenses are estimated at 10% of staff costs. Rent cost for leasing of space for the new pet center has been estimated at $11.00 p.s.f. gross rate on 9000 sq. ft. ($99,000 per year, $8250 per month, escalating at 3% per year.) Recent quotations on available premises range from $9.00 to $14.00 per sq. ft. depending on the quality of the premises and the location. Other annual expenses are in line with current operating costs.

13. Net income before tax is calculated after depreciation and financing charges. Taxes are estimated at 18% of net income.

14. Cash flow projections are based on sales receipts being collected in the same month as the sale. Most sales will be cash or credit card. Credit card discounts have not been included. The cash flow impact of sales taxes collected and paid has not been included as the net effect is near zero. Product costs and operating expenses are projected to be paid in the same month they are incurred.

15. Income taxes are shown as paid at year-end. No dividends are projected in the first five years.

16. The assumed cash flow projections show a need for increased equity financing of $125,000 and corresponding bank loans increasing to $125,000 by the end of Year 1. Loans can subsequently be paid down to meet only the ongoing working capital requirements.

17. Investment requirements are shown for inventory, with receivables at zero (cash only) and capital equipment expenditures are carried   forward to the projected Balance Sheets.

18. Balance Sheet projections show the estimated future assets and liabilities and the growth in Retained Earnings without any dividend payments.

Business Plan - GO Freight Inc.

Purpose

This Business Plan documents the strategies and plans for GO Freight Inc. The primary purpose of this document is to provide potential investors and sources of financing with the information required to evaluate the risks and opportunities associated with this business.

Prepared By: ….., President,

Revised: January 8, 2014
….., Vice-President, Marketing
Copy # ____

Assisted By: Del Chatterson, Consultant

Disclaimer: The management and owners of this business and our consultants make no warranties or representations as to the validity of facts, forecasts and assumptions, or the viability of this plan. The reader is solely responsible for any conclusions or decisions based on the information herein.

Confidentiality and Non-Conflict of Interest: This business plan contains information that is confidential to GO Freight and its owners. It is not to be shared or copied without their prior consent. The reader further acknowledges that he/she has no conflicting personal or business interests in any way related to the planned products or services of GO Freight.

Accepted and receipt acknowledged by:

_____

Signed

_____

Name

_____

Title

_____

Company:

_____

Date

To the reader:

Thank you for your interest in our Business Plan.

In it we present the strategies and plans for the expansion of our business and it must be treated as a confidential document between us.

We are asking you to review this Business Plan for the purpose of your considering participation in the financing of GO Freight. The initial financing of the business has been provided by the current shareholders. Full realization of the business opportunities available will require additional financing as described in this Business Plan.

We appreciate your interest in our plans. Please contact us directly if you have further questions or wish to arrange a follow-up meeting after reviewing the Business Plan.

Yours truly,

President
GO FREIGHT INC.

GO Freight – BUSINESS PLAN

TABLE OF CONTENTS

APPENDICES

1. Executive summary

GO Freight is a new freight services company being launched by two experienced industry professionals with excellent credentials and industry contacts that are already prepared to do business with the new company.

The trucking industry in our area is frequently showing poor levels of performance and customer service and local shippers are ready to consider new alternatives. This situation is creating the opportunity for GO Freight with its knowledge, experience, and contacts to successfully deliver better shipping performance and better customer service. GO Freight will offer traffic management solutions for full truckload shipments, including domestic, import/export, refrigerated trucks, and flat-bed trucks.

GO Freight will focus on delivering services that are cost effective with dependable performance and high levels of customer service. GO Freight will provide transportation management services including the following:

❑ Analysis of traffic patterns to determine specific handling requirements.
❑ Developing least-cost solutions to meet the shipper's needs.
❑ Contracting with the appropriate carriers that will meet the desired service levels for our customers.

The company forecasts sales of $3.4 million in freight revenue in the first year, growing to at least $5 million within five years. Financial projections show this to be a very profitable business opportunity.

In addition to the initial equity investment of $30,000 from the two shareholders, initial bank financing of up to $60,000 is required to support working capital needs, but it is expected to be fully repaid within the first full year of operation.

2. Concept and business opportunity

GO Freight is a new freight services company offering traffic management solutions for overland transportation. This service is known in the freight business as a "third party logistics" company and provides outsourced transport services for a wide variety of shippers requiring inbound and outbound freight services.

GO Freight will focus on delivering specific transportation services that are more effective and economical with higher levels of customer service than companies are otherwise receiving from their internal traffic department or from direct contracting with the trucking companies.

The trucking industry is currently in turmoil due to a variety of factors including the declining manufacturer shipping volumes, the high costs of fuel and consolidation or downsizing among current carriers. The consequence of these distractions for truckers is that both operating performance and customer service are suffering. The effects are evident in missed deliveries, poor customer relations, and low levels of satisfaction for shippers. These conditions are creating an opportunity for our company with the knowledge, experience, and contacts to successfully deliver better shipping performance and better customer service. This is the opportunity being pursued by GO Freight.

The principal owner/managers of GO Freight, ..., and ...., have the necessary expertise and combined experience of more than 30 years in the trucking industry. They know the major shippers and carriers operating in our region and how service and performance can be improved for both parties. Initial feedback from prospective customers that are under-served and carriers that are under-utilized is already very encouraging. (See Testimonials in Appendix ....)

GO Freight see its role of providing expertise and transportation management services to major shippers including the following:
- ❏ Analysis of traffic patterns to determine specific handling requirements.
- ❏ Developing least-cost solutions to meet the shipper's needs.
- ❏ Contracting with the appropriate carriers to meet the desired service levels.

GO Freight will also provide sales representation for carriers from outside our region who do not have representation here to sell their services to local shippers. These carriers are already delivering into the region and have space available for low cost back-hauls that GO Freight can fill effectively and increase their revenues while also delivering cost savings to the shippers.

Specific target markets have been identified that are likely to have stable demand, are generally profitable businesses, and have reasonably complex requirements that offer cost saving opportunities. These industries include:
- ❏ Fresh and frozen food products
- ❏ Horticultural products
- ❏ Health care products
- ❏ Seasonal products

GO Freight will initially limit itself to offering road freight services for full loads, but these will include domestic, import/export, refrigerated trucks, and flat-bed trucks.

An initial forecast for the first full-year indicates a sales potential exceeding $3.4 million based on known customer prospects and their current shipping volumes. Growth in the second year should be at least 20% and then continue to a level of at least $5 million within five years. Financial projections show this to be a very profitable business opportunity and a secure credit risk.

Initial financing will be required in the form of a line of credit to support working capital needs in addition to the initial equity investment of $30,000 from the two shareholders. The total bank financing requirement is expected to rise to an amount of $60,000 during the first two quarters, but is expected to be fully repaid within the first full year of operation.

3. Mission, Vision, Values

GO Freight is committed to becoming recognized as the premier specialist in road transportation for major shippers in our region that require non-standard freight services.

We see ourselves as offering unique expertise and experience that will allow our customers to benefit from cost reductions in their overland freight while receiving exceptional levels of customer service unmatched by our competitors.

GO Freight is also committed to maintaining strong loyalty and dedication from the carriers it uses based on our consistent respect for their requirements, including fair compensation and prompt payment for their services.

Our approach to the market will be through our extensive contact network leveraging our reputations for integrity, competence and dedication to meeting our customers' requirements.

Our approach to management of the business incorporates the principals associated with owner/management and long-term growth of a profitable enterprise. We are dedicated to being successful for our customers, carriers, and employees.

4. Market analysis

The Transportation Market

Supply chain management can be described as supplying the correct product or service, to the correct place, in the correct quantity, at the correct time and at the correct cost.

The National Logistics .... Study, of March 2008, found that supply chain costs represent 32% of the total of manufactured products.

Furthermore, 75% of national corporations of all sizes are encountering difficulty hiring highly qualified logistics personnel, hence the need for outsourcing to experienced logistics managers who can plan and control the efficient movement of goods between shipper and consignee on their customers' behalf. In 2007, the top outsourced supply chain activities were customs brokerage and clearance, freight forwarding, inbound and outbound transportation and warehousing.

In the Logistics / Supply Chain .... National Overview (Sept 2008), research showed that logistics users generally outsourced transportation: 73% of firms outsourced their inbound transportation and 68% outsourced their outbound transportation. Transportation accounts for 85% of the logistics industry revenues estimated at $50 billion. Trucking was the key sub-sector with 42% of the whole logistics industry and 75% of the transportation sector.

This sub-sector is stable and starting to have some differentiation factors due to just-in-time (JIT), and enhanced client demands regarding technology integration. The single greatest potential challenge to the trucking sector in recent history was during the aftermath of the September 11 terrorist attacks in the United States. While inconveniencing cross-border transportation for a number of weeks, the final impact has been more complex and time consuming security procedures that require more expertise and the application of new technology for border crossing truckers.

Target Sectors
GO Freight will focus on this trucking sub-sector and, more specifically, on the full truck-load business. We feel that this strategy will enable us to avoid the distractions commonly encountered by those who enter the market with a wider service offering. Our initial target customers are all financially solid players in stable markets themselves.

The major accounts currently contacted within our target market, our potential revenue rand their total transport business are shown in the table below:

Company	Total Freight Value	% Potential	Revenue Potential for GO Freight
Fruit Co Health Foods Inc.	$$$$	3 %	$$$
XYZ Medical	$$$$	5 %	$$$
Others Inc.	$$$$	7 %	$$$

Customer needs
Customer needs are well understood by the principals of GO Freight and they are also aware of the current deficiencies in performance and customer service. Focusing on meeting those needs, while delivering lower transportation costs, will assure us of attracting, retaining and growing key customer accounts. Maintaining strong, loyal customer relationships is a key element in the sales management plan.

Buying process

In most cases, after an introduction to the services of GO Freight, the shipper will provide enough information on traffic patterns and handling requirements to evaluate their needs and develop a proposal for services. This proposal will be submitted with recommended carriers, routes and the associated costs for comparison by the buyer to current procedures or to alternative submissions. If GO Freight is successful in being the chosen solution then shipping orders will be confirmed by fax, e-mail or telephone.

5. Competition

Third party logistics is a well-established industry offering a variety of services to large multi-nationals and smaller regional companies. The services vary from small package pick-up and delivery to specialty trucking, air and ocean freight, brokerage, warehousing or full logistics management.

Industry characteristics

These services are provided by a wide range of potential competitors for GO Freight. There are large full service companies with a global presence down to local specialists with limited staff and capabilities.

Primary Competitors

Some recognized competitors and their relative market positions are described below:

1. ABC Transport

Started : 1995
Major services: transport, warehousing and distribution
Size: over $10 million in sales
Wide use of technologies including satellite tracking on all company trucks, EDI introduced in January 2001, and other technologies being considered. Service is not consistent or necessarily better because of the technologies. Their service has become so diversified that the fundamentals are being lost, and the latest technologies are not being used to help serve their customers.

2. XYZ Freight

25 years in business
Services include: (in order)
Full-Service Transportation Logistics Carrier and Agency Network
Again, very diversified. Has broken into the LTL market in the past year alone.

3. Logistics Co. Int'l.
Established 1993
Logistics management and warehousing services
Specialize in supplier management, material inventory and procurement and warehousing.

4. Traffic Co.
Established 1986. Very customer-centric. Reps available 24 hours a day by cell. Latest technologies. Divisions started by specializing in vertical markets but have combined into the traditional refrigerated, rail, warehousing. Probably the strongest competition for GO Freight.

5. Logistics Company Inc.
Started 1989.
Started in freight brokering but have added many other services over the years.

In addition to these third party logistics companies, many shippers will assume responsibility themselves and contract directly with individual transport companies. Competition from all these options is recognized and respected. Sometimes customers will remain loyal to their current logistics service providers and some competitors will offer services that GO Freight does not. In these circumstances, there may be no potential business for us.

Nevertheless, our competitors all have weaknesses that lead to performance deficiencies, communications breakdowns and deterioration of customer relationships. These situations all present business opportunities for GO Freight. Our own established customer contacts, our reputation for effective service delivery, and our dedication to constant communication with the customer will allow us to consistently win new business. By focusing on full truckload services and not over-extending our resources, we expect to protect and retain these competitive advantages and build strong, long-term customer relationships with major shippers in our target markets.

6. **Strategic plan**
Background
GO Freight is a legal entity incorporated under the laws of .... in ......, 2007. The company has been registered with the Ministry of Transport as a third party freight services company. Appropriate insurance will be put in place for liabilities and other commercial risks. The company is presently owned 50/50 by .... and .... who will also share management, sales and operations responsibilities.

The strategic objectives and action plan for the business are summarized below.

Strategic Objectives:
1. Open the business and confirm the first major customer commitments by ....., 20__.
2. Complete the first full year of operation with:
   - ❏ Sales exceeding $3,000,000
   - ❏ Profitability demonstrated by before tax income of at least $200,000
   - ❏ Cash flow positive and net debt at zero.
3. Be recognized as an industry leader in third party logistics for truck freight by major shippers in our target markets within three years.
4. Achieve continued, stable, profitable growth to sales exceeding $5,000,000 per year within five years.

Action Plan:
1. Complete a documented Business Plan including financial projections to confirm initial bank financing by ....., 20__.
2. Acquire premises by November 15th and install equipment and services to open for business on December 1st, 20__.
3. Introduce GO Freight to key customer contacts and develop opportunities to commence shipping services in early December.
4. Engage a third employee to assist with administration and customer service at GO Freight to start on December 15th, 20__.
5. Prepare a marketing brochure and web site to promote our services by January 31st, 20__.
6. Achieve the $200,000 in monthly revenue by March 31, 20__.
7. Provide contracted services for at least five major shippers by June 30th, 20__ and add at least one new customer per month until the end of 20__.

These strategic objectives and the action plan with stated goals and milestones will be the planning guide for management through the first year of operations.

7. **Management team**

A primary competitive strength of GO Freight arises from the combined knowledge, skills and experience of its management team. The key members who are dedicated to achieving the company's objectives are:
   - ❏ Name, title, role, responsibilities
     - Summary background ....
   - ❏ Name, title, role, responsibilities
     - Summary background ....

Additional information on each of these individuals is provided in more detail in Appendix B. along with an initial organization structure. Additional experienced resources will be engaged as required. A candidate for the third position as Office Manager has already been identified.

The expected staffing costs are included with the financial schedules of Appendix A.

8.   Service offering

GO Freight will offer traffic management solutions for full truckloads, including domestic, import/export, refrigerated trucks, and flat-bed trucks.

GO Freight will focus on delivering services that are cost effective with dependable performance and high levels of customer service.

GO Freight will provide transportation management services including the following:
- ❏ Audit and analysis of traffic patterns to determine specific handling requirements.
- ❏ Developing least-cost solutions to meet the shipper's needs.
- ❏ Contracting with the appropriate carriers to meet the desired service levels for our customers.

GO Freight will also provide backhaul opportunities from other carriers who do not have representation in our area. These carriers are already delivering into the region and have space available for low cost back-hauls that GO Freight can fill effectively and increase their revenues while also delivering cost savings to the shippers.

9.   Marketing and sales plan

The company has limited plans for marketing activities. The corporate identity and marketing messages will be communicated through a simple marketing brochure and a well-designed basic website. These are already in process so that they will be available to support early sales activities. No direct advertising or publicity campaigns are currently planned other than some listings in trade industry directories both online and in trade publications.

The company principals will maintain their active participation in local traffic clubs, industry associations and transportation conferences and trade shows in order to keep in touch with their contact network and promote GO Freight.

Business development and sales growth will be achieved by continuous direct sales efforts and soliciting leads and referrals from our current customer contacts.

10. **Operations plan**
Location and Facilities
GO Freight will be centrally located commercial offices of the industrial park at
………, ____.

Operating Processes
The services of GO Freight are focused on full truckload freight management for large shippers in our region. Operating processes will be dedicated to providing outstanding levels of customer service by selecting the most appropriate carriers, monitoring performance levels and maintaining constant communication with our customers.

Office systems, information technology and telecommunications will all support those service objectives. Additional staff will be selected, recruited, trained and compensated so that they are also supportive of high levels of performance and customer service.

11. **Risk analysis**
The business risks are understood by management and will be managed to the minimum possible. These risks arise from potential changes in market or economic conditions that are not controllable by GO Freight and from business conditions that are internal to GO Freight and can be minimized.

Market risks:
1. Economic conditions.
   Changes in government regulations, taxes, fees, foreign exchange, interest rates or security requirements will affect all players at the same time and should not provide any competitive advantage/disadvantage.
2. General decline in target markets.
   This risk is limited by the strategy of diversification in various markets and lack of dependence on any single large customer (except for _____ in the first year).
3. New business models, foreign competitors.
   Overland freight is a very hands-on, regional business that cannot be displaced by offshore sources or an online business model.
4. Changes in technology.
   New tools in IT or telecommunications may affect costs, processes, and client expectations but GO Freight is already using the latest technologies available and will keep on top of new tools that may become available.

Business risks:
1. Availability of key personnel
   Partners will sign a shareholders agreement for their mutual protection and acquire key-man life insurance on each other. GO Freight will manage employees to ensure high motivation and retention, but will also take the precautions of having signed confidentiality, non-conflict of interest and non-competition agreements where they are appropriate.
2. Loss of major suppliers
   Protection from interruption of service will be achieved by maintaining alternative freight carriers and other service providers.
3. Systems and facilities risks
   GO Freight will take reasonable precautions to protect systems and facilities and also maintain commercial insurance against business interruption.
4. Regulatory
   GO Freight will maintain all regulatory approvals as necessary.

The financial projections show that GO Freight's business model has strong revenue potential that delivers a high return on investment and is attractive in spite of these known business risks.

12. Financial plan

Initial financial analysis shows that full operating costs can be recovered at a break-even sales level of $ 1.8 million in freight revenue per year. The first year is expected to be almost double that figure.

A detailed financial plan is attached. The Financial Plan includes the following:
- ❏ Opening Balance Sheet and Financial Requirements
- ❏ Sales Revenue and Gross Profit Projections
- ❏ Organisation Plan
- ❏ Expense Forecast
- ❏ Net Income and ROI Projections
- ❏ Cash Flow Forecast
- ❏ Investment Forecast
- ❏ Projected Balance Sheets

This Business Plan has been prepared to describe the business opportunity, the strategy, the operating plan, and the expected financial results.

Thank you for your interest in reviewing our Business Plan.

APPENDICES

A. Financial plan

B. Management team

C. Marketing brochure

D. Market research data

E. Service cost estimates, comparative quotes

F. Letters of reference, testimonials

H. Other relevant documents

Financial Projections – GO Freight Inc.

The financial projections for GO Freight Inc. are shown in the following pages. These example projections will give you some ideas on how to present your own financials. You can then develop spreadsheets to evaluate various scenarios and assumptions, until you are satisfied with the planned results.

Be sure to check your final draft so that the business plan text is consistent with the financial results that you show in your Appendices.

Financial Projections for GO Freight

1. Starting Assumptions
2. Start-up Costs
3. Revenue Forecast
4. Net Income
5. Cash Flow
6. Balance Sheets
7. 5-Year Forecast Summary & Chart

Table 1. STARTING ASSUMPTIONS

REVENUE PROJECTIONS	Units of sale	Sales per Month	Price per Unit	Cost per Unit	Revenue per Month	Gross margin %
1. Standard Freight Contracts	Loads	250	$ 1,000	$ 960	$ 250,000	4.0%
2. Specialty Custom Freight	Loads	75	$ 2,500	$ 2,350	$ 187,500	6.0%
3. Contract services	hours	100	$ 135	-	$ 13,500	100.0%
4.		0	-	-	-	0.0%
5.		0	-	-	-	0.0%

Revenue Growth Forecast	Year 2	Year 3	Year 4	Year 5
	50.0%	30.0%	15.0%	15.0%

Table 2. START-UP COSTS   Future Capital Costs

Capital Equipment	Required to start	Year 1	Year 2	Year 3	Year 4	Year 5
	$					
Office equipment	2,500	0	0	0	0	0
Computers & Software	1,500	1,500	0	0	0	0
Production Equipment	1,500	0	1,500	0	2,500	0
Property & Facilities	500	0	1,500	0	1,500	0
Vehicles & Other	15,000	0	0	0	0	0
Total Start-Up Costs	21,000	1,500	3,000	0	4,000	0

Table 3. REVENUE FORECASTS $1000's

Revenue	Units/mo.	Year 1	Year 2	Year 3	Year 4	Year 5
Sales Growth			50.0%	30.0%	15.0%	15.0%
Standard Freight Contracts	250	$ 2,437.5	$4,500.0	$ 5,850.0	$ 6,727.5	$ 7,736.6
Specialty Custom Freight	75	$ 1,828.1	$ 3,375.0	$ 4,387.5	$ 5,045.6	$ 5,802.5
Contract services	100	$ 131.6	$ 243.0	$ 315.9	$ 363.3	$ 417.8
0	0	-	-	-	-	-
0	0	-	-	-	-	-
Total Revenue: ($1000's)		$ 4,397.3	$ 8,118.0	$ 10,553.4	$ 12,136.4	$ 13,956.9
Cost of Sales:	**% GM**	**TOTAL**	**TOTAL**	**TOTAL**	**TOTAL**	**TOTAL**
Standard Freight Contracts	4.0%	$ 2,340.0	$ 4,320.0	$ 5,616.0	$ 6,458.4	$ 7,427.2
Specialty Custom Freight	6.0%	$ 1,718.4	$3,172.5	$ 4,124.3	$ 4,742.9	$ 5,454.3
Contract services	100.0%	-	-	-	-	-
0.0%	0.0%	-	-	-	-	-
0.0%	0.0%	-	-	-	-	-
Sales Costs, Commissions	2.0%	$ 87.9	$ 162.4	$ 211.1	$ 242.7	$ 279.1
Total Cost of Sales:	$	$ 4,146.4	$ 7,654.9	$ 9,951.3	$ 11,444.0	$ 13,160.6
Average Gross Margin %	%	5.7%	5.7%	5.7%	5.7%	5.7%
Gross Margin: ($1000's)	$	$ 250.9	$ 463.1	$ 602.1	$ 692.4	$ 796.3

Note 1: Monthly Revenue in Year 1 is assumed to grow from 50% in Q1 and 75% in Q2 to 100% of forecast in Q3.

Note 2: Payment and recovery of sales taxes are not included in revenue, expense or cash flow projections.

Table 4

ORGANIZATIONAL PLAN	Year 1	Year 2	Year 3	Year 4	Year 5
NO. OF PLANNED STAFF					
President	1	1	1	1	1
Admin./Acctg.	0.5	1	1	1	1
Sales Manager	0	0	1	1	1
Production and Warehousing	1	2	2	2	2
Freight and delivery	0	0	0	0	0
Customer Service	0	1	1	1	1
TOTAL STAFF	2.5	5	6	6	6
TOTAL STAFF EXPENSE	$1000's	Annual staff expense			
President	69.0	69.0	69.0	69.0	69.0
Admin./Acctg.	20.1	40.3	40.3	40.3	40.3
Sales Manager	0.0	0.0	57.5	57.5	57.5
Production and Warehousing	27.6	55.2	55.2	55.2	55.2
Freight and delivery	0.0	0.0	0.0	0.0	0.0
Customer Service	0.0	17.3	34.5	34.5	34.5
TOTAL STAFF COSTS	**116.7**	**181.7**	**256.5**	**256.5**	**256.5**

Table 5. NET INCOME $1000's

	Year 1	Year 2	Year 3	Year 4	Year 5
TOTAL REVENUE	$ 4,397	$ 8,118	$ 10,553	$ 12,136	$ 13,957
Average $ Revenue/Employee	**1759**	**1624**	**1759**	**2023**	**2326**
Cost of Sales (Excl. Labour):	4,146	7,655	9,951	11,444	13,161
Gross Margin: ($1000's)	251	463	602	692	796
Average % Gross Margin	5.7%	5.7%	5.7%	5.7%	5.7%
OPERATING EXPENSE	-	-	-	-	-
Staff Costs	117	182	256	256	256
O/H and Admin Exp.	24	46	46	46	46
Sales & Mktg Exp.	12	12	12	12	12
Operating Expense	152	239	314	314	314
Operating Expense % of Sales	3.5%	2.9%	3.0%	2.6%	2.2%
OPERATING PROFIT (EBITDA)	**99**	**224**	**288**	**378**	**482**
% Operating Profit	2.2%	2.8%	2.7%	3.1%	3.5%
Interest Current Loans 6.50%	1	1	1	1	1
Interest-New Funds 8.50%	2	2	2	1	0
Depreciation 15.00%	2	4	3	3	3
NET INCOME BEFORE TAX	**94**	**217**	**282**	**373**	**478**
Taxable Income	94	217	282	373	478
Income taxes payable	18	41	54	71	91
NET INCOME AFTER TAX	**76**	**176**	**228**	**302**	**387**
% NET INCOME AFTER TAX	**1.7%**	**2.2%**	**2.2%**	**2.5%**	**2.8%**
Return on Total Assets	0.3	0.3	0.2	0.2	0.2
Return on Shareholders Net Worth	1.7	1.0	0.6	0.5	0.4
ESTIMATED BUSINESS VALUE: @ 3 x Net Income after tax of Year 5 = $ 1,162,269					

Note:
1. Interest rates on financing are applied to the loan balances shown in the Cash Flow Forecast.
2. Taxes are calculated on a base rate of 19%, applying any tax loss carry-forward from prior years.
3. Business valuation is a very rough estimate of future business value at three times the forecast Net Income after Tax in Year 5.

Table 6. CASH FLOW FORECAST $1000's

	Year 1	Start	Year 2	Year 3	Year 4	Year 5
Initial cash balance	4	0	535	2143	5003	8462
Sales receipts	3951		7895	10148	11873	13653
Additional sources	0		0	0	0	0
CASH INFLOW	3951	0	7895	10148	11873	13653
Cost of Sales	2778		5129	6667	7667	8818
Operating Exp.	152		239	314	314	314
Capital Costs	2	21	3	0	4	0
Add to Receivables	446	0	670	879	1011	1163
Add to Inventory	0	0	5	5	5	5
Interest - Current	1		1	1	1	1
Interest - New funds	2		2	2	1	0
Dividends paid	0		0	0	50	100
CASH OUTFLOW	3382	21	6049	7869	9054	10401
SURPLUS/SHORT	569	-21	1846	2278	2818	3253
ADDITIONAL FUNDS						
Add to Acc. Payable	294	0	444	582	665	761
Bank Line of Credit	0	0	0	0	0	0
Other Loans	0	0	0	0	0	0
Shareholder loans	0	0	0	0	0	0
Shareholder Capital	0	0	0	0	0	0
New Financing	0	25	0	0	-25	0
NET CASH FLOW(+/-)	531	4	1608	2860	3459	4013
CUM. CASH BALANCE:	535	4	2143	5003	8462	12475
Bal. Current Loans	20	20	20	20	20	20
Bal. New Financing	25	25	25	25	0	0

Notes:
1. Sales receipts are partially received in the following quarter and expenses are all paid in the current period.
2. Increases in Accounts Receivable, Inventory and Payables affect cash flow and the Year-end Balance Sheet.
3. The payment and refund of sales taxes are assumed to have no net effect on operating cash flow.

Table 7. PROJECTED BALANCE SHEETS

	Opening Balance Sheet	Year 1	Year 2	Year 3	Year 4	Year 5
ASSETS			$1000's			
Cash*	4.0	-55.2	40.0	194.3	366.9	596.2
Other current	1.5	0.0	0.0	0.0	0.0	0.0
Accounts Receivable	1.5	446.5	669.7	879.5	1,011.4	1,163.1
Inventory	15.0	15.0	20.0	25.0	30.0	35.0
Depreciated Capital Cost	21.0	22.5	23.8	20.2	21.2	18.0
Less Depreciation	0.0	1.7	3.6	3.0	3.2	2.7
Net Capital Assets:	21.0	20.8	20.2	17.2	18.0	15.3
TOTAL ASSETS	43.0	427.1	750.0	1,115.9	1,426.3	1,809.6
LIABILITIES						
Accounts payable	2.5	296.9	444.0	581.8	665.1	761.0
Bank Line of Credit	20.0	20.0	20.0	20.0	20.0	20.0
Other current	1.5	1.5	1.5	1.5	1.5	1.5
New Financing	25.0	25.0	25.0	25.0	0.0	0.0
Shareholder Loans	25.0	25.0	25.0	25.0	25.0	25.0
Shareholder Capital	8.0	8.0	8.0	8.0	8.0	8.0
Cum. Retained Earnings	0.0	75.8	251.5	479.6	731.7	1,019.1
Shareholders' Equity	8.0	83.8	259.5	487.6	739.7	1,027.1
TOTAL LIABILITIES	82.0	427.1	750.0	1,115.9	1,426.3	1,809.6

* Balancing entry.

Table 8. SUMMARY – GO FREIGHT FINANCIAL PROJECTIONS

5-YEAR FORECAST	Year 1	Year 2	Year 3	Year 4	Year 5
Total Revenue	$4,397	$8,118	$10,553	$12,136	$13,957
Gross Margin	$251	$463	$602	$692	$796
GM % of Sales	5.7%	5.7%	5.7%	5.7%	5.7%
Operating Expense	$152	$239	$314	$314	$314
Exp. % of Sales	3.5%	2.9%	3.0%	2.6%	2.2%
Operating Profit	$99	$224	$288	$378	$482
Profit % of Sales	2.2%	2.8%	2.7%	3.1%	3.5%
Net Income	$76	$176	$228	$302	$387
Net Income % of Sales	1.7%	2.2%	2.2%	2.5%	2.8%

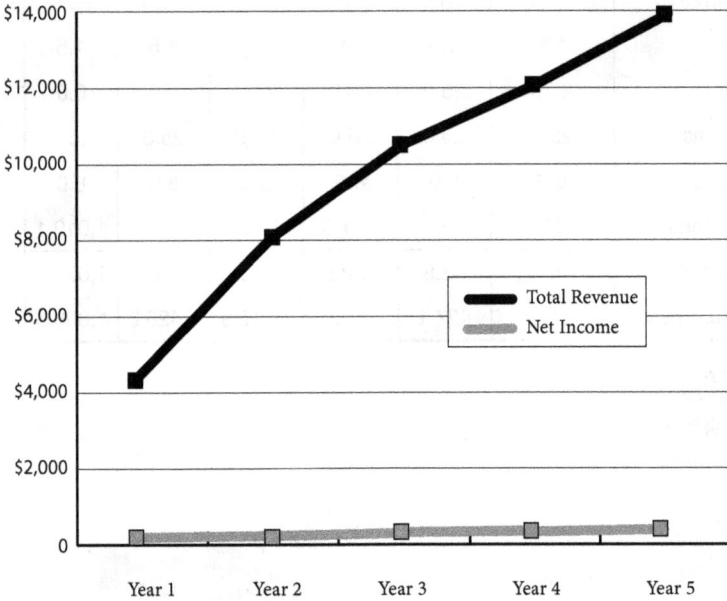

THE EXIT

Your business should be built with the exit in mind.

If you follow the principles discussed in Chapters 11 and 12 of this Guide to Business Plans you will manage your business and its reported financial results so that you will be prepared to sell at any time.

These examples of Offers for Sale of a business will give some guidelines for the relevant presentation documents when you are ready to exit.

Think of them as your most likely last Business Plan.

Boxco Packaging – Manufacturing Business for Sale

Business for Sale

CONFIDENTIAL DOCUMENT

SUBJECT TO A NON-DISCLOSURE AGREEEMENT

WITHOUT PREJUDICE

FOR DISCUSSION PURPOSES ONLY

Boxco Packaging Ltd.

Dated: October __ th, 20__

Background

Boxco Packaging is a manufacturer and distributor of packaging products in business since 1982. The company is owned and managed by the two shareholders.

The owners are nearing retirement and planning to exit the business in the near future. Their current objective is to realize fair cash value for their equity in the business and to arrange an orderly transition to new ownership that will successfully continue to operate, serve customers and grow the business.

Business Description

❑ Locations: Manufacturing, offices and warehouse facilities are located in _____.

❑ The company owns the building and property (estimated market value at $1.3 million), currently occupied only by Industrial Boxco. Total available space is 25,000 sq. ft. with manufacturing and warehousing of 20,000 sq.ft. on the ground floor and offices of 5000 sq. ft. on the second floor.

❑ Most products are sold under the BOXCO™ brand name, which has been widely recognized for packaging products for over 15 years.

❏ Industrial Boxco also manufactures packaging for private labels and supplies raw materials for their in-house packaging products.

❏ Sales are well diversified over a variety of industries, products and applications with approximately 30% of shipments to European customers. Less than 40% of sales are to the U.S. Both domestic and export markets have important opportunities for future growth.

❏ The company and the BOXCO brand name have an established reputation for high quality, innovative and cost effective packaging products and reliable, knowledgeable, personalised customer service.

❏ The top three of over 100 active customers accounted for 38% of sales in the first five months of last year; the top 8 were at 65% of sales.

❏ In the last year over two million products were shipped with 450 different part numbers (SKUs) were shipped for $1,085,000 in sales. There were only twenty items at more than $20,000 in sales each and another 15 items of over $5000/year each. In total, the top 50 items (11.1% of items sold) accounted for about $639,000 (58.7%) of total sales.

❏ Current production capacity and equipment allow in-house manufacturing of all products. The company is operating well below its production capacity and could deliver over 200% sales growth without any significant investment in capital equipment.

❏ Production staff (8 – 10 employees) are experienced, stable and loyal to the company.

❏ Sophisticated and comprehensive management information and accounting systems, including an online e-commerce application are in place and are well supported and maintained.

Acquisition Opportunity

A knowledgeable and competent purchaser with the ability to manage the business and grow sales revenues will realize the following benefits and achieve a high Return on Investment with the acquisition of the Industrial Boxco business:

❏ Annual Operating Income (EBITDA) available to shareholders is projected to exceed $500,000 per year at annual sales of $3.0 million per year.

❏ Cost reductions resulting from integration with existing resources and infrastructure in management, production and distribution.

❏ Rapid growth in revenue from the sale of complementary products to existing customers.

❏ Expansion of sales by leveraging available marketing and sales resources, particularly in the U.S.

❏ Expansion into new and under-developed markets with more aggressive promotion and development of the BOXCO brand name.

❏ Access to the existing e-commerce site, information systems and production and distribution facilities that are capable of handling a larger integrated operation with much higher sales volumes.

Summary Financial Information
(Based on year-end reports at Sept. 30th)

INDUSTRIAL BOXCO	REPORTED FINANCIAL RESULTS						
Year-end Aug.31	2015	2016	2017	2018	2019	Average 5-YEARS	Avg. % of Sales
Revenue (Total Sales)	$1,312,709	$1,332,861	$1,525,572	$1,084,902	$1,241,153	$1,299,439	Prior 5-Yr.
Material Costs	$ 508,419	$ 488,315	549,132	307,516	437,273	458,131	35.3%
Direct Labour	$ 231,838	$ 240,819	258,996	239,703	214,392	237,150	18.3%
Manufacturing Overhead	$ 206,035	$ 206,516	194,545	187,691	167,140	192,385	14.8%
Cost of Sales	$ 946,292	$ 935,650	1,002,673	734,910	818,805	887,666	68.3%
Gross Profit	$ 366,417	$ 397,211	522,899	349,992	422,348	411,773	31.7%
Average Gross Margin %	27.9%	29.8%	34.3%	32.3%	34.0%	31.7%	
Operating Expense	$ 140,239	$ 140,518	137,967	113,656	120,594	130,595	10.1%
Net Income (Before Tax)	$ 226,178	$ 256,693	384,932	236,336	301,754	281,179	21.6%
Income tax	42,974	48,772	73,137	47,103	59,182	54,234	4.2%
Net Income after Tax:	$ 183,204	$ 207,921	311,795	189,233	242,572	226,945	17.5%
Interest Expense:	$ 7,998	$ 7,313	5,282	3,414	1,636	5,129	0.4%
Depreciation Expense	$ 26,887	$ 21,619	17,363	14,766	14,576	19,042	1.5%
Adjusted EBITDA	$ 261,063	$ 285,625	$ 407,577	254,516	317,966	305,349	23.5%
% EBITDA/Sales	19.9%	21.4%	26.7%	23.5%	25.6%	23.4%	
Net Inc. from E-Commerce Business	$ 15,000	$ 23,477	$ 20,000	$ 12,331	$ 12,000	16,562	1.3%
Combined EBITDA	$ 276,063	$ 309,102	427,577	266,847	329,966	321,911	24.8%
AVAILABLE NET CASH FLOW (Adjusted Net Inc. + Deprec.)	$ 225,091	$ 253,017	349,158	216,330	269,148	262,549	20.2%

Net Worth:

- ❏ Current Book Value of Equity: $ 824,287
- ❏ Estimated Realizable Value of Equity
(With all assets adjusted to Current Market Sale Values): $ 2,700,000

Amounts above do not include owner/management discretionary income, paid as dividends. All figures are subject to confirmation based on Accountants Review Financial Statements to August 31, 2014 for both companies.

Sales Terms & Conditions
- ❏ Selling price is $2,500,000 to acquire 100% of the equity in the operating business of Boxco Packaging.
- ❏ Purchaser of equity will acquire all assets, including the building and property (but not including surplus cash on-hand and invested funds) plus current liabilities, proprietary technology, equipment and process innovations, customer lists and goodwill including a recognized brand name and registered trademark.
- ❏ Minimum down payment of 20% and balance payable in cash over 6 to 18 months.
- ❏ Shares to be held in escrow until paid in full (control rests with the current shareholders until they are paid in full).
- ❏ The two owners are willing to remain available full-time for a minimum six months with a management contract at reasonable compensation for each. After six months, management contracts may be negotiated for the time required with appropriate compensation as mutually agreed.
- ❏ If the building and property are not included in the sale, the purchaser will be required to sign a minimum 5-year net/net lease at current market rates for the property, building and facilities.

Note:
1. Additional information will be provided for interested and qualified buyers to perform due diligence under non-disclosure, non-compete and non-conflict of interest, subject to acceptance of the prospective buyer's Letter of Intent to commence negotiations for acquisition of the business and confirmation of financing within 60 days.
2. All terms and conditions are subject to negotiation and to subsequent review by the respective party's lawyers and financial advisors to assure that the intended tax consequences, warranties and liabilities are appropriately documented.

Service Co. Inc. – Professional Services Business for Sale

Service Co. Inc.

CONFIDENTIAL DOCUMENT

SUBJECT TO A NON-DISCLOSURE AGREEEMENT

WITHOUT PREJUDICE: FOR DISCUSSION PURPOSES ONLY

Discussion Points for Merger/Acquisition

Dated July 7th, 20_.

Following is a summary of the background, strategic objectives and potential for a mutually beneficial merger or acquisition for Service Co. Inc.

Background

Service Co. Inc. is currently 100% owned by Ms. W____ who is the only executive and is solely responsible for business management, sales growth and profitability. She is planning for management succession and transfer of ownership of the business over the next three to five years to allow for her exit from full-time management and to realize the maximum cash value of her equity investment in the business.

Ms. W ____ is the President, CEO and the most senior and experienced consultant in a team with five other consultants and one part-time administrative assistant. A recent organisation review has confirmed that no internal candidate is sufficiently qualified to assume the role of President or General Manager of the business. Consequently, we are pursuing opportunities for a merger or acquisition that would add experienced management talent and ensure the continuity of Service Co. after the departure of Ms. W____.

Objectives

❏ To enhance the business value and ensure continuity by adding an experienced and well-qualified partner to assume senior management responsibility for financial performance and business development.

❑ To transfer knowledge and responsibilities over the next two to three years to allow the gradual exit of Ms. W____.

❑ To ensure both protection of the value of equity and shareholder income during the transition period.

Business Description

❑ Service Co. Inc. provides professional consulting services related to regulatory approvals and quality assurance for food products in Canada.

❑ The company currently leases 2500 sq. ft. of fully serviced office space at

_____.

❑ Clients are primarily manufacturers and distributors including both small businesses and large multi-nationals who are seeking assistance to introduce new food products and grow revenues in Canada.

❑ Sale revenue is stable and well diversified with many loyal, long-term clients in all sectors of the industry.

❑ Last year Service Co. had total sales revenue of $715,000 and revenue of $675,000 in the previous year. Projected sales are running at $740,000 for the current year.

❑ In the past three years, Service Co. has done business with twenty-four different corporate clients. The top three clients accounted for 72% of sales in the past year compared to 63% in the prior year. The top seven clients ranged in annual sales revenue from $218,000 to $12,000 each.

❑ Sales revenue was approximately __% in regulatory affairs and ___ % in quality assurance.

❑ The potential consulting revenue with higher utilisations rates for the existing staff of seven employees is estimated at $1,200,000 per year.

❑ Comprehensive management information and accounting systems and supporting infrastructure are in place and are well supported and maintained.

Acquisition Opportunity

An established and experienced strategic partner from the consulting industry will realize the following benefits to achieve a high Return on Investment from an acquisition or merger with Service Co. Inc.:

❏ Revenue growth to $1,200,000 in annual sales within two years with the addition of an experienced senior executive or business partner responsible for client relations and business development.

❏ Cost reductions from integration and merging of resources and infrastructure in business management and client relations.

❏ Expansion of the customer list and of the services and resources offered.

❏ Access to the shared knowledge base, customer data base and project history for more effective sales efforts and delivery of services.

❏ Availability of experienced, skilled and bilingual professional consultants.

Summary Financial Information
(Based on year-end reports for Dec. 31ˢᵗ, for past years plus estimates of future years.)

REPORTED FINANCIAL RESULTS							
Service Co. (Year-end Jan.31)	2010-11	2011-12	2012-13	Average Last 3 Years	% of Sales	Medium Term Potential	% of Sales
Revenue (Total Sales):	$ 628,696	$ 625,241	816,328	752,443	100%	1,200,000	100%
Cost of Sales	$ 2,014	$ 38,857	45,792	42,597	5.7%	65,000	5.4%
Gross Profit	$ 626,682	$ 586,384	770,536	709,845	94.3%	1,135,000	94.6%
Average Gross Margin %	99.7%	93.8%	94.4%	94.3%		94.6%	
Administration Expense*	$ 688,014	$ 407,804	509,175	471,392	62.6%	690,000	57.5%
Financing Costs	$ 13,742	$ 14,063	7,511	7,504		7,500	0.6%
Total Operating Expense	$ 701,756	$ 421,867	516,686	478,895	63.6%	697,500	58.1%
Net Income (Before Tax)	$ (75,074)	$ 164,517	253,850	230,950	30.7%	437,500	36.5%
Income tax (Projected @ 16%)	$ -	$ 6,343	48,195	39,478	5.2%	70,000	5.8%
Net Income after Tax	$ (75,074)	$ 158,174	205,655	191,472	25.4%	367,500	30.6%
Interest Expense	$ 13,742	$ 14,063	7,511	7,504	1.0%	7,500	0.6%
Depreciation Expense	$ 14,385	$ 12,594	8,995	7,998	1.1%	12,500	1.0%
EBITDA (Earnings before Interest, Taxes, Deprec. & Amortization.)	$ (46,947)	$ 191,174	$ 270,356	246,452	33.1%	457,500	38.1%
EBITDA/Sales %	-7.5%	30.6%	33.1%	32.8%		38.1%	0.0%
NET CASH FLOW (Net Inc. + Deprec.)	$ (60,689)	$ 170,768	214,650	199,470	26.5%	380,000	31.7%
Owners' Discretionary Cash Payout (Bonus + Dividends)	$ -	45,000	160,000	170,000		350,000	

Proposed Terms & Conditions

- ❏ Owner's current valuation of equity is $1,500,000 for 100% of the shares in Service Co. Inc.

- ❏ An acquisition or merger will be expected to be based on an agreed valuation model using current financial results and an agreed formula to be applied to future results to establish pricing of subsequent transactions between the parties.

- ❏ Purchasers of equity will have shares held in escrow until paid in full (control rests with the current owner until more than 50% are acquired and paid in full).

- ❏ The owner expects to remain in an executive position full-time for a minimum of two years with a management contract at reasonable compensation in line with historical discretionary payout. After one year, the management contract may be re-negotiated with time and compensation as mutually agreed.

Note:

1. Additional information will be provided for interested and qualified buyers to perform due diligence under non-disclosure, non-compete and non-conflict of interest, subject to acceptance of a prospective buyer's Letter of Intent to commence negotiations for acquisition of equity in the business and subject to confirmation of financing within 30 days.

2. All terms and conditions are subject to negotiation and to subsequent review by the respective party's lawyers and financial advisors to assure that the intended tax consequences, warranties and liabilities are appropriately documented.

Sample NDA (Non-Disclosure Agreement)

The following is an example of a Non-Disclosure Agreement (NDA) that might be applicable for parties in negotiations that require disclosure of confidential company information.

Please note that it is included here for illustration purposes only and it is not offered as legal advice applicable to any particular jurisdiction.

MUTUAL AGREEMENT of NON-DISCLOSURE

NON-COMPETITION & NON-CONFLICT OF INTEREST *

CONFIDENTIAL

THIS AGREEMENT effective as of _____ th, 20__ by and between:

Company A. Inc.

Address:_____

And

Company B. Inc.

Address: _____

WHEREAS:

Company A. Inc. and Company B. Inc. have expressed a mutual interest in advancing negotiations for the transaction under discussion and subsequently doing business together, and

For this purpose, either party may from time to time disclose information to the other party that is proprietary in nature and confidential to the disclosing party.

NOW THEREFORE in consideration of the covenants and promises herein contained,

THE PARTIES HERETO AGREE AS FOLLOWS:

1. In this Agreement, "Confidential Information" means all proprietary information of either party that is communicated by one party to the other pursuant to this Agreement concerning the business of either party and/or their related or affiliated entities, which information is non-public, confidential and/or proprietary in nature.

2. Each party agrees to treat the Confidential Information disclosed to it as confidential, proprietary information of the other party and agrees not to disclose to others such Confidential Information or make mention of the discussions between the parties, except as provided herein.

3. The parties agree that they will use the Confidential Information solely and exclusively for the purpose of the proposed negotiations. Notwithstanding the generality of the foregoing, the parties agree that they will not use the Confidential Information, or any part thereof, for their own purposes.

4. Further, the parties agree that there is no current Conflict of Interest in receiving the confidential or proprietary information and that they will not seek or incur Competitive Advantage from receipt of this information.

5. The parties will utilize at least the same degree of care to avoid unauthorized disclosure of Confidential Information provided to them as a careful and prudent business person would use to protect his or her own confidential information from unauthorized disclosure.

6. The parties undertake to limit access to the Confidential Information to only those employees or professional associates and advisors of their respective companies or affiliated companies who need access thereto for purposes of this Agreement and who have agreed to these confidentiality obligations. Prior to releasing the Confidential Information to such employees or third party advisors, the receiving party shall issue appropriate instructions to satisfy its obligations under this Agreement.

7. Neither party will copy or reproduce any written Confidential Information provided to it without the prior written consent of the disclosing party.

8. Nothing in this Agreement will apply to Confidential Information which:

    (a) is known to a party prior to being disclosed by the other party, provided such prior knowledge is documented in written records or publications which are in the receiving party's possession or can otherwise be demonstrated to have been known to the receiving party prior to such disclosure;

(b) is rightfully obtained in good faith by a receiving party from any third party who had no confidentiality obligations to the disclosing party;

(c) is available to the public in the form of a printed publication (electronic or otherwise) or patent, or to any third party without restrictions as to its confidentiality;

(d) is developed by a receiving party independently of any disclosure under this Agreement; or

(e) is required to be disclosed by judicial or administrative process, provided that the receiving party will promptly notify the disclosing party and allow the disclosing party reasonable time to oppose such process.

Confidential Information will not be deemed to be within the foregoing exceptions if it is specific and merely embraced by more general information in the public domain or the receiving party's possession, or it is a combination, which can be reconstructed by piecing together information from multiple sources, none of which shows the whole combination, its principle of operation or method of use.

9. The parties acknowledge and agree that nothing herein creates any commitment whatsoever concerning a possible relationship between the parties.

10. This Agreement is not intended to create, and shall not be construed as creating, a joint venture, partnership or other form of business association between the parties.

11. The parties agree that they would not have an adequate remedy at law and would be irreparably harmed in the event that any of the provisions of this Agreement were not performed by the other party in accordance with their terms or were otherwise breached by the other party. Accordingly, the parties agree that they may be entitled to injunctive relief to prevent breaches of this Agreement and to specifically enforce the terms and provisions hereof in addition to any other remedy to which they may be entitled at law or in equity.

12. This Agreement constitutes the entire understanding between the parties with respect to Non-Disclosure, Non-Competition and Non-Conflict of Interest. All additions or modifications to this Agreement must be in writing and must be executed by both parties.

13. If any provision or any part of this Agreement is or held to be unenforceable, invalid or illegal, then it shall be severable and deemed to be deleted, and the remaining provisions of this Agreement shall remain valid and binding to the full extent permitted by law.

14. This Agreement will be governed by the laws of the Province/State of _____ and, where applicable, the federal laws of the country of _____.

IN WITNESS WHEREOF the parties hereto have executed this Agreement, effective as at the date set out above.

Company A. Inc.:

Signed By: _____

Name: _____ Title: _____

Company B. Inc.:

Signed By: _____

Name: _____ Title: _____

*Note: This sample Non-Disclosure Agreement is meant for illustration purposes only and does not constitute legal advice or a recommendation for use. It has not been reviewed or approved by any legal authority and should not be considered as applicable to any particular situation without appropriate legal review.

Additional Resources Used and Recommended

During the course of preparing various Business Plans for myself or clients and while writing this Do-It-Yourself Guide, I have accessed many other resources which I recommend to you for additional insights and information to help you prepare a successful business plan that gets the results that you want.

You will also find input to consider that may complement my advice in this Guide and that may be more relevant to your specific needs.

GUIDES AND TEXTBOOKS

Check at your local business school, university or collage library and you will find certainly find useful references on business management and leadership, entrepreneurship and business planning.

Additional business planning guides may be available from your accountant or bank and check what your friends and colleagues recommend. After you have recommended The Complete Do-It-Yourself Guide to Business Plans to them, of course.

ONLINE RESOURCES

Most banks, business consulting firms and other professional organisations offering services to entrepreneurs provide online access to strategic planning, business plan guides, checklists, outlines and even templates. They are easy to access and explore.

You will also find vendors of software tools that can be purchased and downloaded to "automatically" prepare a business plan from your input. These I do not recommend. They are usually a poor fit to your specific plan and very difficult to adapt to your circumstances. Output always looks computer-generated from a "fill-in-the-blanks" form and will not be well received as your own business plan. An overly polished and formatted plan lacks authenticity in representing your unique ideas and your approach to starting and building a viable business.

My final word is to review alternative resources for a broader perspective on what is required and how to prepare a suitable business plan.

But keep it simple. Make it yours.

And do it yourself.

A Personal Note to Readers

Thank you for taking the time to consider my advice and recommendations for preparing a business plan and using it for the purposes you have in mind. Either to get started on your business with all the necessary resources and financing in place, or to provide better leadership and strategic direction to your business management and growth plans, or to arrange for your exit from the business by selling it to new owners. I hope it really does help you get the results you want.

The Complete Do-It-Yourself Guide to Business Plans is one of two business books for entrepreneurs that I am publishing in 2020. The other book of advice from your Uncle Ralph is titled, **DON'T DO IT THE HARD WAY**. Both books were originally published in 2014.

If you are interested in stories about entrepreneurs, in addition to advice for entrepreneurs, you may enjoy reading and sharing my Dale Hunter Series of crime fiction novels about a young entrepreneur in the computer business of the 1980s fighting crime and corruption to save his family and his business. The first three novels in the series were published in 2018 and 2019: NO EASY MONEY, SIMPLY THE BEST and MERGER MANIAC.

In all my writing, I use storytelling as the best way to share my experience, advice and ideas to help entrepreneurs do better and be better. And to generate a little more sympathy and understanding for entrepreneurs. I sincerely believe they are capable of making a significant positive contribution to society in spite of the popular negative stereotype of the greedy, selfish and irresponsible entrepreneur. Enlightened entrepreneurs work hard to be better and do better for themselves and their families, their employees, customers and suppliers, their communities and the planet.

All of my writing tries to meet those multiple objectives – to inspire and promote enlightened entrepreneurship.

I hope you enjoy the books and recommend them to your friends. Please share your review comments with me and other readers. It helps us all to make better decisions about what to read and what to write.

You're also invited to visit my websites and join the newsletter mailing lists for the Reader Review Panel or for Ideas for Entrepreneurs to keep in touch and receive advance notice of my next writing projects. Please visit: **DelvinChatterson.com** or **LearningEntrepreneurship. com** to sign up.

Many thanks for your continued interest and support of my writing. Enjoy your reading and learning.

Your Uncle Ralph,

Del Chatterson

Montreal, Canada,
March 2020

Acknowledgements

This Guide is made more valuable, and interesting and useful, thanks to the input of all the clients, consultants, bankers, business partners, investors and associates that I have worked with during the last thirty years and more.

I could not possibly name them all. Some may recognize themselves in the real life stories and examples that I have used in the Guide and I apologize if they remember it differently or if I neglected to mention all the lessons we learned together.

I also appreciate and respect all the feedback and suggestions from readers, friends and associates on the earlier editions. They have contributed immensely to making this 2020 Edition a better Guide to Business Plans.

The quality of this publication has been greatly enhanced by the active support and professional services of my book cover and interior designer Rodolfo Borello and the publishing, printing, e-commerce and fulfilment services delivered by Canam Books/ Rapido Press.

And most importantly, thank you to my infinitely patient wife, Penny Rankin, who used to be suspicious of entrepreneurs and has now supported and encouraged me through every revision.

Thank you all!

Your Uncle Ralph,

Del Chatterson
Montreal, Canada,
March 2020

The Author, Delvin R. Chatterson

Del Chatterson is dedicated to helping entrepreneurs to be better and to do better.

He is an experienced business advisor, consultant, entrepreneur, executive, writer and cheerleader for entrepreneurs. Through his consulting business, **DirectTech Solutions**, and his website at **LearningEntrepreneurship.com**, Del provides ideas, information and inspiration to business owners, managers and entrepreneurs.

Originally from the Rocky Mountains of British Columbia, Del has lived and worked for most of the past forty years in the fascinating, multicultural, bilingual, French-Canadian city of Montreal, Quebec. Del has helped entrepreneurs around the world, including volunteer consulting and financial support in developing economies and in Indigenous communities. His own life experience includes running nine marathons after the age of fifty (setting no records, but never being last) and running for Member of Parliament in the 2000 Canadian federal election. (He came second, not last.)

In addition to his business books, Del is also writing fiction with the Dale Hunter Series of crime thrillers about an entrepreneur in Montreal in the computer business of the 1980s (Not his true life story. It's mostly fiction, he says.) He is also working on a collection of short stories and continues to Blog and post regularly on social media and his websites.

Del has helped businesses at all stages: from start-up through to the operating and management challenges of achieving sustainable growth and profitability and the exit strategies for management transition and succession plans. His expertise is most often applied in assessing business performance and developing strategic plans to achieve higher levels of performance and profitability.

Del has lectured at Concordia and McGill Universities on entrepreneurship, financial management and business planning. He has given seminars and workshops on business management and entrepreneurship issues and continues to offer his advice for entrepreneurs through his Blogs, articles and books under the persona of your Uncle Ralph.

Del Chatterson is an engineer from the University of British Columbia with an MBA from McGill University. He started a computer products distribution business, called TTX Computer Products, in 1986 and grew it to $20 million a year in sales with distribution centres in Montreal and Boston in just eight years. He then took it into a merger to expand the business across Canada. The merger was eventually wound up as the computer industry rapidly evolved to become more concentrated around a few major players and Del transitioned to the new economy of Internet and Web based businesses.

Del is a resource to business managers and entrepreneurs in a wide array of businesses for his strategic insights, perceptive assessments and insightful analysis of business performance and for defining action plans to realize the opportunities for improvement.

You can learn more about Del at his author website: DelvinChatterson.com and more of his advice for entrepreneurs at: LearningEntrepreneurship.com. You may also follow him on Twitter, Facebook, Instagram, or LinkedIn.

Thank you for sharing his books and providing your feedback, comments, and reviews. Del welcomes any opportunity to connect with his readers, fans and friends.

www.ingramcontent.com/pod-product-compliance
Lightning Source LLC
Chambersburg PA
CBHW071606210326
41597CB00019B/3421